BEST PRACTICES:

Difficult People

WORKING EFFECTIVELY WITH PRICKLY BOSSES, COWORKERS, AND CLIENTS

JOHN HOOVER

D0193464

Collins

An Imprint of HarperCollinsPublishers

HarperCollins books may be purchased for educational,
business, or sales promotional use. For information,
please write: Special Markets Department, HarperCollins
Publishers, 10 East 53rd Street, New York, NY 10022.

Produced for HarperCollins by:

HYLAS PUBLISHING
129 MAIN STREET
IRVINGTON, NY 10533
WWW.HYLASPUBLISHING.COM

FIRST EDITION
Library of Congress Cataloguing-in-Publication Data has
been applied for.

ISBN: 978-0-06-114559-9
ISBN-10: 0-06-1145559-9

07 08 09 10 11   RRD   10 9 8 7 6 5 4 3 2 1

John Hoover is a former executive with Walt Disney Productions and McGraw-Hill and holds master's degrees in marriage and family therapy and in human and organizational development, as well as a Ph.D. in human and organizational systems. Dr. Hoover is a leadership coach, organizational communications specialist, organizational behavior consultant, workshop leader, and keynote speaker for organizations, including the American Society of Training and Development, the Boeing Leadership Center, Delta Air Lines, IBM, Motorola, the New York State Training Council, the Society for Human Resource Management, Xerox, and many others.

He is also the author and coauthor of 12 management and motivation books, including *Bullwinkle on Business: Motivational Secrets of a Chief Executive Moose, How to Work for an Idiot, How to Live with an Idiot, How to Sell to an Idiot, The Art of Constructive Confrontation, Unleashing Leadership, Leadership When the Heat's On* with Danny Cox, and *Time Management* in the Collins Best Practices series.

Contents

Preface

Why are some people so difficult to work with? What's the best way to deal with them? How can you cope with a boss who's a Slave Driver or a Bully? What about the colleague who shows up repeatedly in your office to chat about personal matters? Why are some managers able to take difficult people in stride, while others feel overwhelmed by them? How do you avoid becoming a difficult employee?

In this book, we distill the wisdom of some of the best minds in the field of human resources to help you manage difficult people—perhaps one of the most challenging problems of the workplace. The language is simple and the design colorful to make the information easy to grasp.

Quizzes help you assess your knowledge of difficult people and how to handle them diplomatically. Case files show how people have managed difficult people effectively. Sidebars give you a big-picture look at the challenges inherent in managing a group with diverse personalities and highlight innovative, out-of-the-box solutions worth considering. Quotes from business leaders, psychologists, and human resources experts will motivate you as you interact daily with difficult people. Finally, in case you want to dig deeper into the literature of difficult people and management, we recommend some of the most important business books available. The authors of these books both influence and reflect today's thinking about handling difficult people effectively and related management issues. Understanding the ideas they cover will inspire you as a manager.

Even if you don't dip into these volumes, the knowledge you gain from studying the pages of this book will equip you to deal firmly, effectively, and insightfully with the difficult people you face every day—to help you make a difference to your company and in the lives of the people who support you.

THE EDITORS

HOW DIFFICULT PEOPLE AFFECT THE WORKPLACE

"My main job was developing people. Of course, I had to pull out some weeds, too."

—Jack Welch,
former CEO of General Electric and author of *Winning*

From line supervisors to senior managers, today's leaders are in the business of developing their people, which means helping them develop strong and productive relationships. Your challenge as a manager is to form coalitions of willing, eager, and ambitious people within your realm of responsibility.

Self-Assessment Quiz

ARE DIFFICULT PEOPLE TAKING A TOLL ON YOU?
Read each of the following statements and indicate whether you agree or disagree. Then check your score and study the analysis at the end.

1. I have difficult people reporting to me.

    ○ Agree   ○ Not Sure   ○ Disagree

2. I must work with difficult coworkers.

    ○ Agree   ○ Not Sure   ○ Disagree

3. I report to a difficult person as my boss.

    ○ Agree   ○ Not Sure   ○ Disagree

4. My subordinates take up too much of my time.

    ○ Agree   ○ Not Sure   ○ Disagree

5. My coworkers take up too much of my time.

    ○ Agree   ○ Not Sure   ○ Disagree

6. My superiors take up too much of my time.

    ○ Agree   ○ Not Sure   ○ Disagree

7. People who take up my time are "difficult."

    ○ Agree   ○ Not Sure   ○ Disagree

8. Difficult people make me unproductive.

    ○ Agree   ○ Not Sure   ○ Disagree

9. Difficult people make their peers unproductive.

   ○ Agree   ○ Not Sure   ○ Disagree

10. Difficult people cost my organization money.

   ○ Agree   ○ Not Sure   ○ Disagree

Scoring

Give yourself 2 points for every question you answered "Agree," 1 point for every question you answered "Not Sure," and 0 points for every question you answered "Disagree."

Analysis

15–20   You believe that difficult people are disruptive and that they waste time and other resources. Difficult people are a serious issue for you.

10–14   You aren't sure whether or not difficult people are a problem for you, for other people, or for your organization as a whole. You have thick skin or are in denial.

0–9   You aren't convinced that difficult people are problematic. You are either right or oblivious to what's happening around you—in which case you may be a difficult person yourself.

Getting in your way, when you least expect or have the time to deal with them, will be difficult people.

If you observe enough managers over time, you'll notice that some are far less annoyed than others by these problematic employees. That's not because frazzled managers have a greater number of difficult people on their staff or that their difficult people are so much more challenging. Rather, serene managers have developed better skills for dealing with difficult people.

Every difficult person that you come into contact with is an opportunity for you to grow and develop into a stronger, more resilient—and more serene—manager. Fortunately, the coping skills you need can be learned.

THE COST OF DIFFICULT PEOPLE

The exact cost of difficult people in the workplace is incalculable. Examining the subject is like trying to watch a skyscraper being built by peering through a knothole in a plywood construction fence. You are only able to see a portion of the complete picture at any given time.

The problem is not only that difficult people make everyone miserable, but also that they diminish your effectiveness and the effectiveness of those around you. Your effectiveness is a measure of how you get things done on time, under budget, with quality workmanship, and without overturning any apple carts, so that you get positive performance reviews, promotions, and raises.

Behind the Numbers

THE NEGATIVE MATH OF DIFFICULT PEOPLE

Difficult people often cause turnover, either because the difficult person decides to leave, is terminated, or causes the departure of someone else. According to one study on the effects of the U.S. Family Medical Leave Act, "Turnover costs for a manager average 150 percent of salary, including tangible costs of hiring new workers and relocation, and intangible costs such as the new worker's inefficiency and lost productivity while the job is vacant." When you do the math using this formula, here's how much it costs to replace employees at the following salary levels:

Existing employee's salary:	$35,000
Cost of replacement:	$52,500
Existing employee's salary:	$50,000
Cost of replacement:	$75,000
Existing employee's salary:	$65,000
Cost of replacement:	$97,500
Existing employee's salary:	$75,000
Cost of replacement:	$112,500

SOURCE: "How Much Does Employee Turnover Really Cost?" by Will Helmlinger, *Inc. Magazine* (January 2006).

Difficult People Undermine Your Authority

If you have institutional authority as a supervisor, manager, director, or higher executive, there is probably a difficult person over whom you have some control. A difficult person can

> "Just estimating the number of hours wasted each week, and then multiplying that figure by the hourly salary of the employees involved, doesn't cover all the costs of a difficult employee. Difficult employees are contagious, spreading unanticipated consequences throughout the organization."
>
> —Patricia Wiklund, author of *Taking Charge When You're Not in Control*

Behind the Numbers

COMPLAINING COSTS TIME AND MONEY

By their own admission, employees waste valuable time complaining about their bosses. Thirty-one percent of the employees polled by badbossology.com and the international leadership development firm Development Dimensions International said they spend more than 20 hours per month complaining about or listening to others complain about their bosses. Twenty-eight percent complained for 10 hours a month, 29 percent for three hours, and 12 percent for 30 minutes. That time spent sniping is all wasted.

SOURCE: "Bad Bosses Drain Productivity," *T + D Magazine* (November 2005).

undermine your popular authority—that is, the leadership role you've earned among the people you work with through your consistent and trustworthy behavior. A difficult person can complain about you when you're not present, compete with you for power, impede your ability to follow through on promises, and so on. If the difficult person misrepresents what you have done or how effectively you do things in general, it will become that much harder for you to build people's faith and trust in you—the very foundations of your popular authority.

Difficult People Waste Your Time

Chances are you never seem to have enough time to do everything your job requires. Difficult people can make it even harder. Some require your attention and focus. Some cause problems among peers that require your time to mediate. Some are unable to do their jobs, forcing you to deal with getting the job done.

Red Flags ✕◆

HOW OTHERS INFLUENCE YOU

How do people you work with impact your effectiveness? One way is by making excessive demands on your attention. It's difficult to be effective at your job when you're spending all your time dealing with others. It's important to recognize when one person is causing you and your team to become less productive. Some questions to consider:

- Is the person wasting his own time?

- Is he wasting others' time?

- Is he wasting company money or resources?

Difficult People Bring You Down

A difficult person can indirectly affect the overall success of a whole department or company. When there is dissention in your ranks or among your peers, the losses in energy, enthusiasm, and productivity diminish results in ways that are difficult to quantify. Team efficiency suffers if you and your subordinates simply avoid the person causing the problems. Information gets lost when people don't communicate. The weak spots in your departmental efforts will create points of dysfunction and disconnect with customers and other departments. As problems mount, your reputation as an effective leader and team player will suffer, and your whole department will feel the consequences. The mud slide of problems sucks the vitality out of your workplace and saps the energy that you and your best people owe to your jobs.

Difficult People Affect You at All Levels

The effects of difficult people vary depending on whether they are coworkers, subordinates, or your boss.

Difficult subordinates affect your ability to get your job done. Doing their work as well as your own doesn't solve the problem; it simply drains energy and focus away from your own job.

Difficult coworkers can withhold cooperation and support and can undermine your popular authority. Whether or not you're considered a team player is determined largely by the quality of your interaction with others. Difficult lateral relationships can be costly in hidden ways.

If your boss is difficult and you handle the situation clumsily, you could wind up being labeled difficult yourself—a label that you might not shake for the rest of your career.

Stay or Go?

In reaction to difficult people, some workers leave—only to find a new batch of difficult people in their new position. Whether you stay or go, you need to learn how to cope. The truth is that difficult people are everywhere.

Many people prefer to stay and work with someone who might drive them bananas but is

Dos & Don'ts ☑

STAYING ON AN EVEN KEEL WHEN FACED WITH DIFFICULT COLLEAGUES

As you attempt to address the problems that working with difficult people can cause, remember these tips:

☐ Do read what your peers write, listen to what they say, and observe what they do.

☐ Don't ignore what happens around you because it is not in your direct line of fire.

☐ Don't arbitrarily write off negativity or boss bashing—try to figure out the cause.

at least predictable. There is much to be said for knowing what to expect from someone, even if it's unpleasant. Yet a manager who is truly driven by the desire to create a better organization—one that is a good workplace for its employees and a valuable provider of goods and services for its customers—will try to address the problems difficult people introduce in the workplace.

WHY ARE DIFFICULT PEOPLE SO DIFFICULT?

As a general rule, the problems you encounter in dealing with a difficult person stem from

☐ Do jump on opportunities to communicate with your colleagues.

☐ Do contribute to newsletters, positive blogs, and group activities.

☐ Don't forget your manners—never say or write anything about someone else you wouldn't want that person to hear.

☐ Do learn to be a good buffer between your superior and your subordinates.

☐ Don't join forces with subordinates against your boss.

one of two sources: conflicting expectations or unclear boundaries.

Conflicting Expectations

Although personality conflicts, political differences, or something as simple as disagreement over how high the office thermostat gets set can cause friction, the underlying difficulty is often misaligned expectations. For example, John is not meeting Mary's expectations and he is angry about it. Never mind that the two of them have never discussed their mutual expectations to begin with!

> "An expectation is a resentment waiting to happen."
>
> —Old saying

When you expect something from someone else—increased sales, stepped-up performance, higher productivity, or more help with your workload—you set yourself up for the possibility of disappointment. Offices are full of subordinates, coworkers, and superiors walking around resenting each other over expectations they never discussed, negotiated, or agreed to. Subordinates, peers, and superiors become "difficult" when they stand between you and your expectations.

Subordinates tend to expect that you are going to somehow make everything right in their world.

The BIG Picture

CATCH-22

Many people job-hop because they are fleeing difficult peers or, more often, difficult bosses. They're hoping, of course, that they will get to work with more amiable peers or bosses in their new situations.

According to the United States Department of Labor, young people entering the workforce today are likely to change jobs seven to ten times in their careers. Although people move for many reasons—to seek better compensation and opportunity, to move to another part of the country, or because their jobs are outsourced—many people change jobs to get away from difficult people. What they find in their next job is more difficult people. And so they continue hopping from job to job in search of the utopian workplace.

Unfortunately, difficult people are everywhere. In today's workplace, you just have to learn to get along with them to succeed.

Outside the Box

NO ISOLATION WITHIN ORGANIZATIONS

Don't ever think that you are working in isolation where your subordinates or coworkers are concerned. Always connect with people in ways that make them feel better about what they're doing. To become a positive topic of conversation, you need to be seen as someone who truly helps other people, both subordinates and peers, achieve their goals. If coworkers perceive you as difficult, imagine what is said about you when you're not around.

When you make an effort to support and advocate what your organization needs, it reflects well on you. The support of your colleagues positions you to make a positive contribution to your company.

It's an unreasonable expectation, yet it came with your promotion. Subordinates complain about being micromanaged yet resent it when you don't give concise and clear directions. If you give concise and clear directions and they don't follow through, they may still blame you.

Your peers' expectations can also be unreasonable. Jobs and job responsibilities shrink or expand depending on the person and her appetite for work. The problem is that no two individuals share the same appetite for work.

This variability sets the stage for unrealistic expectations among peers. If you expect all people to invest the same amount of effort in their jobs as you do, you're likely to be disappointed. Or, turning the tables, your coworkers might

> "Dealing with people is probably the biggest problem you face, especially if you are in business. Yes, and that is also true if you are a housewife, architect or engineer."
>
> —Dale Carnegie,
> author of *How to Win Friends and Influence People*
> (1888–1955)

expect you to pick up the slack when they cause a problem, without ever admitting that they caused it. If you complain, you are difficult. Just because your coworkers' expectations aren't reasonable doesn't keep them from resenting you. Your boss may expect you to put in the same 60 to 80 hours of work per week that she does. Or she may have unreasonable expectations in terms of your productivity. She may expect you to know how to do certain tasks you have not been taught to do. Often, resentment results from unrealistic expectations that are simply based on a lack of awareness.

The fastest and simplest way to deal with the resentment that arises from unrealistic or unfulfilled expectations is to confront it head on. Usually, people naturally take their resentments to friends, comrades, or anyone they feel will be sympathetic toward them. The one person they don't go to is the one they're having trouble with. And yet he or she is the only person who can offer a solution.

If you feel someone resents you because of expectations you've set for them—or you resent someone such as your boss or coworker for expectations they've set for you—talk to them. Resentments tend to evaporate when they are discussed. As long as conversations about expectations remain constructive, most people become less difficult once they feel they know the score. Both of you can more easily accept what you do or don't do if you are up front about it.

But you must be the one to initiate the conversation—the other person is unlikely to approach you. Sometimes people get so frustrated that they give up. They may stop trying to communicate and begin to ignore or avoid you. Especially if you are dealing with a difficult subordinate, it is your responsibility to make sure that you are speaking each other's language.

Disregarded Boundaries

One very reasonable expectation that we all have of others is that they respect our physical and emotional boundaries. Even people who are otherwise easy to get along with can become irritated and impatient when someone oversteps their boundaries. Understanding the concept of boundaries can be particularly important in the workplace.

Boundaries can be physical or emotional—that is, what you will and will not tolerate in the way others treat you or talk to you. People who cross

THE COST OF WINNING AN ARGUMENT
The cost of not knowing how to deal with a difficult person can be huge. Win the battle over who is right with coworkers and you could lose the war when you need their cooperation and support the most. If you insist on being "right" with your boss, you could pay even more dearly. Being right may feel good in the moment. But the next moment, you may be watching advancement opportunities and even your position disappear. Sometimes it's better to suppress your feelings and simply put an argument on hold, or agree to disagree—and then move on.

THE BOTTOM LINE

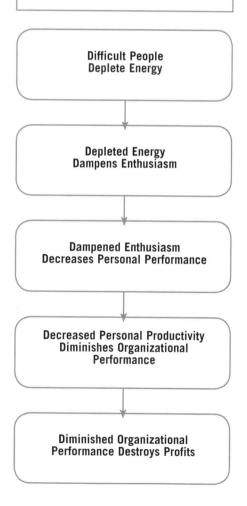

WORK **FLOW** TOOLS

THE CHAIN REACTION OF DIFFICULT PEOPLE'S EFFECTS ON THE WORKPLACE

Difficult People
Deplete Energy

Depleted Energy
Dampens Enthusiasm

Dampened Enthusiasm
Decreases Personal Performance

Decreased Personal Productivity
Diminishes Organizational
Performance

Diminished Organizational
Performance Destroys Profits

these boundaries without permission can seem difficult. For example, a subordinate crosses your boundaries when he walks into your office uninvited, cuts you off in meetings, sends out department-wide directives without consulting you, or makes unauthorized purchases. He becomes a classic difficult subordinate. Or a competitive coworker at or near your same level on the organization charts ventures into your territory. He becomes a classic difficult coworker.

Some people will test you at every turn, even creating opportunities to see how far they can go. Enforcing your boundaries, without going to the extreme of shutting people out entirely, is important if you intend to earn popular authority with peers, subordinates, and even superiors in your company. A reputation for getting walked all over won't earn anyone's respect. The alternative—keeping to yourself—won't ingratiate you with your group or organization either. The middle ground is to be politely assertive.

It can be even more challenging to deal with a boss who seems oblivious to the boundaries to which you are entitled—a reasonable amount of privacy, autonomy, and self-direction in doing your job. Although he may feel that his authority gives him carte blanche, a trusting relationship can't develop if you are constantly worried about him popping up in your physical or emotional space without warning. Moreover, your problems with your boss can spill over into your relationship with your subordinates.

You have the authority to enforce boundaries as the head of your group or department.

Doing so can help you avoid difficult behavioral problems. Enforcing boundaries that make sense to people and help build and maintain a comfortable working environment will eliminate confusion and embarrassment.

"Every business everywhere is staffed with imperfect human beings and exists by providing a product or service to other imperfect human beings."

—Bob Parsons,
CEO of GoDaddy.com

Finding a Solution

Difficult people in the workplace set off a chain reaction of negative consequences that spare no one. It's impossible to put a price tag on, but rest assured it is expensive.

Being the one who initiates the solution to problems that result from unrealistic expectations or unclear boundaries is one of the fastest ways to gain popular authority among those you work with—and to help you become more effective as a leader and a manager. The next chapter discusses several distinct categories of difficult people and gives you strategies and language to deal with them.

UNDERSTANDING DIFFICULT PEOPLE

"Your job is not to do all the work yourself or to sit back and wait to 'catch [your people] doing something wrong' but to roll up your sleeves and help [them] win. If they win, you win."

—Ken Blanchard,
author of *The One Minute Manager*

Most of us work with people who could be considered "difficult," often without really understanding what makes them so irritating. Largely, that's because they get under our skin and engage our emotions and, once that happens, it's hard to be objective.

Self-Assessment Quiz

PROBLEM VERSUS SOLUTION

This quiz will help you understand how you look at the issue of difficult people in the workplace. Choose the answers below that best describe you.

When I encounter a difficult person at work, I:

1. [A] compare myself to that person to see who is right
   [B] walk the other way as fast as possible
   [C] pause for a moment to reflect on why I find the person difficult.

2. [A] determine which of us has more authority within the company to use against the other
   [B] avoid all contact with that person
   [C] purposely have more casual contact with that person to see if I'm getting the whole picture.

3. [A] determine which of us has more authority among the staff to use against each other
   [B] plot how I can defend myself against any and all use of authority against me

[C] study how institutional and popular authority issues can help build a bridge between us.

4. [A] keep score of his crimes against me
   [B] try to pretend there is no friction
   [C] think about what's bothering me and try to understand why I find this person's actions so irritating.

5. [A] find out which subordinates are on my side
   [B] assume all my subordinates are against me
   [C] assume all my subordinates are friendly and reasonable until they prove otherwise.

6. [A] find out which coworkers are on my side
   [B] assume all my coworkers are against me
   [C] assume all my coworkers are friendly and reasonable but might have their own issues to deal with.

Self-Assessment Quiz

7. [A] find out which superiors are on my side
    [B] assume all my superiors are against me
    [C] consider that whatever is causing the person difficulty might have nothing to do with me.

8. [A] quickly strategize how to attack first
    [B] quickly dig a bomb shelter and crawl into it
    [C] strategize how to remove all misunderstandings.

9. [A] get in his face as a warning not to mess with me
    [B] run and tell my boss that I'm being harassed
    [C] treat the other person with respect regardless of how he treats me.

10. [A] find some people who seem to be neutral about the difficult person and go to lunch to talk about the situation
    [B] cut off all contact with that person and use all of my influence to cut off her resources
    [C] invite the difficult person to lunch to find common ground.

Scoring

Give yourself 2 points for every A answer, 1 point for every B answer, and 0 points for every C answer.

Analysis

15–20 You're aggressive and too quick to play the blame game. You may lack the skills and temperament to deal with difficult people in a collaborative way. Use aggressiveness to solve the problem, not to attack the person, or you risk becoming difficult.

8–14 You deal with conflict by avoiding it. You assume the worst, build defensive walls, and avoid confrontation. You tend to deny that you could be part of the problem.

0–7 You seek solutions and see people for their potential rather than regarding them as problems. You prefer collaboration to conflict. You make an effort to improve your communication and cooperation with others at every level of the organization.

Once we're provoked and begin to react emotionally, our productivity as workers and leaders diminishes, and our perception becomes distorted. We might be convinced that the person is the problem, but in most cases it's something the person is doing—their behavior—that's really driving us nuts.

To begin to understand the phenomenon of difficult people, this chapter examines ten of the most common difficult behaviors, discussing how the behavior shows up in the workplace, exploring the "why" behind the behavior, and giving step-by-step instructions for dealing with the problem. The better you understand the essential nature of difficult people and what makes them tick, the more effective your response can be.

As you read through the chapter, keep in mind that some difficult people may fall into several categories. Such complex composite personalities can seem impossible to deal with at times. Some are more challenging than others. In every case, patience is essential for coping. It takes time and careful observation to pinpoint the problems. It also takes time for the methods and techniques you apply to take hold and begin to improve your relationship with the difficult person.

Focusing on improving the relationship is important because you can't reasonably expect to change a difficult person—you can only hope to influence and change his behavior. Your power lies in your willingness to alter your own assumptions and attitudes. When you take the initiative, you reap the rewards.

THE SLAVE DRIVER

SOMEONE WHO MAKES UNREASONABLE
DEMANDS ON YOUR TIME, RESOURCES,
AND ATTENTION

Slave Drivers are almost always people you
report to. Who else has the authority to make
huge demands on you? The demands themselves may vary: Slave Drivers may expect you
to accomplish enormous amounts of work
in incredibly short time frames, or they may
simply want you to spend vast amounts of
time working. They may expect you to achieve
results (such as an exponential increase in
sales) that are simply beyond reason, or they
may expect you to put your personal life aside
for the sake of the business. When it becomes
impossible to keep up with the pace or the sheer
volume of work, you know you are dealing with
a Slave Driver.

What Makes the Slave Driver Tick?

Understanding why this person is putting pressure on you will help you find an effective way to
deal with him. In most cases, people who make
unreasonable demands do so for one of three
reasons: They're overloaded themselves, they're
unaware of the impact of their demands and are
therefore unrealistic about what you can do, or
they're just plain passing the buck.

It's possible that the Slave Driver is actually
a slave to someone else who is piling on the
work—the very work that is cascading down
onto you. It may also be that the Slave Driver's

ambition is pushing him to take on more than one person can reasonably handle. If the Slave Driver isn't able to fulfill his promises, the pressure may wind up on you.

A "clueless" Slave Driver may never have done your job and may not understand the time and energy it would take to produce results at the requested level. It is easy for people to make assumptions and hold unrealistic expectations. A clueless Slave Driver may not be aware of the other claims and constraints on your time.

Finally, some bosses simply consider it executive privilege to hand over their work to those below them. When you are asked to do both your own work and that of your boss, your job becomes nearly impossible. Bosses who pass the buck in this manner are the most difficult Slave Drivers to deal with.

Dos & Don'ts ☑

THE SLAVE DRIVER

If you have discovered that there is a Slave Driver in your midst, there are ways to deflect the added undue stress a Slave Driver's hard-to-meet expectations and demands bring.

☐ Do approach the Slave Driver in a positive and helpful way.

☐ Do observe how he manages his workload, then try to put it in perspective.

What You Can Do About Slave Drivers

No matter what the reason for the Slave Driver's behavior, your approach must always be to be positive and helpful; you want to be part of the solution—not part of the problem. Anything you do takes courage. But the alternative is worse. You will either be exhausted from the work or criticized if you don't complete it—or complete it but do an inadequate job. Unfortunately, when you don't deal with the situation, it can become even worse.

The Overloaded Slave Driver

To relieve some of your boss's burden and pre-pare yourself and your direct reports for what's coming, study how your boss manages his work-load. Make notes about his workload: Where is it coming from and when? Does it fluctuate wildly from light to heavy? Is it a steady stream? Is it

☐ Don't hesitate to clarify how the extra work can negatively affect the overall productivity of your department.

☐ Do sit with him and write up a plan to deal with overwhelming workloads.

☐ Don't forget to distribute work evenly among staff members so that no one person gets bogged down.

predictable or unpredictable? Develop methods to anticipate what future demands will be like so you're not continually taken by surprise.

Then help the Slave Driver put his workload and yours in perspective. Make it clear to your boss how the extra work ripples into your department or area and impairs your efficiency. Brainstorm ways that your boss can be better prepared for what's coming, not take on so much, or possibly fend some of it off.

Finally, write up a plan to deal with the work. Plan to finish the most important items first—don't waste time and energy giving equal time

Outside the Box

YOU'RE NEVER NOT COMMUNICATING

In their book *The Pragmatics of Human Communication,* Paul Watzlawick, Janet Beavin, and Don Jackson wrote, "One cannot not communicate." Their point is powerful: People above, below, and all around you in the organization are paying attention when you least expect them to and don't seem to be paying attention when you most want them to. They are paying attention to the words you speak and the words you choose not to speak. They see what you do and are aware of what you could have done but chose not to do. They note your attitude and the resonance or dissonance your attitude has relative to your words and actions.

to everything. If some things fall off the list so that your life can return to normal, make sure they're not important. Throughout, be positive and helpful. Support your boss and your staff.

The Clueless Slave Driver

If your Slave Driver is completely unrealistic about what you can handle, or is generally unaware of what you're experiencing, become an educator. Explain what an optimal workload would be in your department and what the effects of overload are. Then work with the Slave Driver to schedule work in a way that you both

When you're considering what makes people difficult and how to deal with them, think about what they are communicating—even when they think they are not communicating. Difficult people are sending you an endless stream of clues. Your challenge is to read them properly. Consider which causes the most difficulty: expectations people have of you or expectations you have of other people? It should be evident if you're paying attention to the communication that's never not happening.

SOURCE: *The Pragmatics of Human Communication* by Paul Watzlawick et al. (W. W. Norton, 1967).

Behind the Numbers

THINKING A LOT OF HIMSELF

How good are you at getting along with others? Psychologist David G. Myers asked a group of men to rate their "ability to get along with others." Here's what they thought:

- 25 percent believed they got along with others better than 99 percent of the population did.

- 60 percent believed they got along with others better than 90 percent of the population did.

- 0 percent, amazingly, believed their ability to get along with others was below average.

While most people apparently assume they are better than others at dealing with people, few actually deal well with difficult people. Employees need to be aware of how they interact and how others perceive them.

SOURCE: *In Search of Excellence* by Thomas J. Peters and Robert H. Waterman, Jr. (HarperCollins, 1982).

agree is more realistic and practical. Before that happens, gather data about how the quality of work deteriorates when people are overloaded. Remain positive and helpful.

The **BIG** Picture

DON'T TURN A BLIND EYE

Some people with difficult attitudes appear to be unimportant in the scheme of things, and you might be tempted to ignore them. However, just because someone lacks the social or professional skills to get along with others doesn't mean that they can't make a positive contribution to your department—a contribution that might even further your career.

As a manager or coworker, you might have a great deal to gain from making an extra effort to approach, talk to, and come to build a positive working relationship with a person everyone else has labeled "difficult." Sometimes people with difficult personalities are exceptionally intelligent or gifted with numbers. Sometimes they're innovative and good at thinking outside the box. Or they might be instinctive, analytical problem solvers—if only someone would ask. If you turn a blind eye to these folks, you might be losing a lot.

Begin by comparing the Slave Driver's expectations and your job description. Write down what you and your staff must do on a daily basis. How heavily does the extra workload burden you and your people? What are

the financial and operational consequences of
constant overwork? Note what the best working processes would be for you and your staff
and plot out a reasonable range of workload

• POWER POINTS •

RESCUE AND EDUCATE YOUR SLAVE DRIVER

Slave Drivers demand 150 percent. To
deal with them effectively, keep the
following things in mind:

- Slave Drivers are often overworked
  themselves.

- Slave Drivers often don't understand your job.

- Slave Drivers may dump their work
  on you because they don't want to
  work hard.

- Find out how you can help your
  boss if he is a Slave Driver.

- Keep your Slaver Driver boss
  informed about your workload.

- Document all requests for extra
  work and note how the extra work
  affects the quality of your output
  and your performance.

fluctuations from high to low. Figure out how to tell when overworked people are reaching the point of diminishing returns and beginning to make costly mistakes. Discuss all this information with your boss and jointly write up a plan to reschedule the workload in the best way possible.

Distribute work evenly among staff members. Monitor and document how much is being accomplished, who is doing the work (even if it's just you), and how much time it takes, so that the Slave Driver understands exactly what is required to accomplish what is being demanded.

The Over-Delegating Slave Driver

If your Slave Driver likes to dump and run, start by documenting your own workload and that of your staff. Then note how the additional work overtaxes you, creating mistakes and causing delays.

Put the Slave Driver's work back on his chair. On top, place your analysis of the workload logjam and—while remaining positive and cooperative—ask to meet to review the work together to determine priorities.

Be constructive. Slave Drivers usually respond cooperatively when confronted with evidence that the work is excessive.

Don't be critical. With the Slave Driver's involvement, if possible, write up what is to be done first, second, and third and make sure he signs off on the revised priorities in case anybody asks how you arrived at them.

THE BLACK HOLE

SOMEONE WHO TAKES EVERYTHING YOU CAN
GIVE AND THEN ASKS FOR MORE

This difficult person can be your boss, a peer, or
a subordinate. Like the imploded star that sucks
in all kinds of matter never to be seen again,
the Black Hole personality relentlessly demands
approval, time, and attention and distracts you
from your own work. No matter how much help
and support you offer, it's never enough.

HOW TO HANDLE ALL BASIC CONFLICTS

According to communications scholars
Gerald Miller and Mark Steinberg, there
are three basic types of interpersonal
conflict or reasons people find one another difficult. In *pseudo conflict,* people
actually agree with each other but, due
to misunderstandings, they appear to
each other to be disagreeing. In a *simple
conflict,* people genuinely disagree over
which course of action to take. In *ego
conflict,* people believe they are being
personally attacked. In dealing with all
types of interpersonal conflict:

• Ask the people involved to clarify their
  perceptions.

What Makes Black Holes Tick?

Black Holes may be key people in your department or area. So you can't just ignore them, especially if you are in a position of authority. In fact, Black Holes are interested in you precisely because of your stature.

Black Holes are often insecure people who lack confidence in their work, their social prowess, or their judgment. They constantly question their worth and accomplishment. Even if they are intelligent, talented, and resourceful, they don't

- Let them express their grievances.

- Forbid personal attacks.

- Establish a supportive rather than defensive climate.

- Discourage people from "battling it out" or working it out on their own.

- Be sure the issues are clear to everyone involved.

- Remain calm and unemotional.

- Take notes on what the person says he wants and expects, and date your notes.

SOURCE: *Between People* by Gerald Miller and Mark Steinberg (Science Research Associates, 1975).

THE BOTTOM LINE

believe it. So at every stage, they ask you to check their work. Every project requires more time and takes you away from your own work.

Black Holes often question whether they are accepted among their peers. The fact is that people distance themselves from Black Holes to avoid their clinging behavior; their fear of rejection is a self-fulfilling prophecy. Black Holes feel isolated and worry about their work relationships rather than their work.

What You Can Do About Black Holes

The best way to counteract the distracting behavior of Black Holes who lack confidence in their professional abilities is to take an active interest in their work. If you can build up their confidence, they'll stop looking to you for help all the time. Here's how to begin:

Take the initiative. Start the conversation yourself. Stop by the Black Hole's work station and talk about what she's doing. This way, the conversation is on your schedule, not hers. The sooner you take the initiative, the sooner she'll stop showing up in your doorway.

Each time she asks you to weigh in about her work, make a note of what stage the project is in. It's very possible that she may be stuck, waiting for the project to be explicitly or tacitly "approved," rather than moving on to the next stage of the project.

Encourage her to move forward. Give her benchmarks (or, in the case of peers, suggest them) and clearly define how the work should progress. When you do this, you are giving the

Black Hole permission to move forward—in anticipation of your approval. Then begin the conversation again from the top.

> "Leaders must articulate a vision for everyone and not get caught up in managing munutiae. Involve everyone and welcome great ideas from everywhere. It just might be the quietest person on your team who is sitting on the best idea."
>
> —Jack Welch

Bring her into the group. You don't want a Black Hole who lacks confidence in her social skills to feel isolated, especially if she is the keeper of important information or has contributions to make. Although you can't change her attitude about herself, you can affect how she acts at work. Start by praising her work and asking for her permission to share her work with others. You can do the show-and-tell yourself or

Dos & Don'ts ☑

MANAGING A BLACK HOLE

If you give your Black Hole positive feedback and clear concise directions, you may find her becoming more productive. Many Black Holes are in need of on-the-job guidance that only takes a moment to provide.

☐ Do take an active interest in her tasks and projects.

☐ Do encourage her to move on when she sufficiently completes a task.

☐ Do invite her input on others' work as a way of showing that you value her opinions.

☐ Don't forget to document her__ increasing decision-making skill and independence.

☐ Don't let a good call go unnoticed.

have her do it. The fact that you are providing an opportunity for her to receive approval from her peers will boost the Black Hole's confidence.

Similarly, invite the Black Hole's input on the collaborative work that others do. Tell her publicly that her input and opinions are important. Give her increasingly visible positions based on her work, challenging her to top herself in presentations. She will feel safe knowing you are behind her. Draw her into interactions with others in groups. Remind her of her successful track record in public interaction as a means of encouraging more.

Build confidence. Encourage the Black Hole to have more confidence in her decision-making. Revise her job description, with her agreement, to include independent decision-making as part of the job. Schedule regular conversations to discuss her progress in this area.

Invite the Black Hole into your decision-making process: "I need your help making this decision." Then be sure to use her input and praise her publicly: "So-and-so and I made the decision." Black Holes frequently are talented people whose input will benefit you greatly. So facilitating their involvement is a win-win situation. Challenge the Black Hole to make increasingly bigger decisions.

Then, use specific vocabulary to support her decisions. "Good decision" is a powerful message. "I like that decision" also works. "That's going to produce exactly the results we need" is another opener.

Finally, document her increasingly responsible decision-making and remind her regularly of the progress she's making. Show her a map of how this work led to that work, which ultimately made the other thing possible, all as a result of her responsible decision-making. Don't let any good call go unrecognized.

None of this is to say that the Black Hole should become a major project and consume all your time. This is simply good leadership and a smart way to turn a difficult situation around for the better.

Your choice is clear: You can pro-actively and skillfully engage the Black Hole in the same way that you build up and encourage any subordinate, peer, or superior—or you can allow her to engage you on her terms, which will swallow up too much of your time and energy.

THE MINUTIAE MONSTER
SOMEONE WHO IS INEFFICIENT, UNFOCUSED, AND OBSESSED WITH DETAILS

Minutiae Monsters are time wasters, known for being indecisive, getting tangled up in details, and straying off course. In meetings, they're the ones who want to know how many widgets are attached to the thing-a-ma-jig when everyone else is focused on the big picture. Their obsession with details can be valuable—but only if it is controlled. If not, Minutiae Monsters will never get anything done or realize their potential to be strong contributors at work. When you need them, they will still be at the starting line, preoccupied by the fine points or busy doing something irrelevant.

What Makes the Minutiae Monster Tick?
The Minutiae Monster has never met minutiae he didn't like. Before making a decision, he will pore over every last detail, consider every option, and spend countless hours weighing potential outcomes. Sometimes the obsession with details

Dos & Don'ts ☑

DETAILING THE MINUTIAE MONSTER

Getting hung up on small details is typical of Minutiae Monsters. There are myriad reasons why they are snagged so easily by details that are seemingly unimportant. Like the Black Hole, the Minutiae Monster is genuinely interesting in doing things the right way but may lack the ability to discern what's most important.

☐ Don't focus on eliminating his preoccupation with details.

☐ Do help him build the skill necessary to become more organized and focused on the big picture.

☐ Don't underestimate the importance of the little details that contribute to major changes or decisions.

☐ Do reward the Minutiae Monster for assignments and tasks done in a timely fashion.

☐ Don't forget to emphasize that timeliness is just as important as making the correct decisions.

☐ Do team up Minutiae Monsters with colleagues who are highly organized and productive.

Red Flags ⚑◆

WATCHING FOR WALLS

Difficult people's true feelings are often kept under cover. To deal with them—and to manage effectively—you must be aware of what's going on around you, even when people throw up walls. You don't need to be paranoid. Just stay tuned in to what might be concealed. Watch out for trouble spots such as:

- People withholding critical information from other groups and from you

- Groups of subordinates and peers bonding and spending an unusual amount of time together

- People asking why they aren't in the information loop

- Differences of opinion occurring between groups with different tenure, expertise, and politics

- People watching for others' reactions at meetings

- A person talking a lot in private but rarely in meetings, keeping important information hostage is deceptive; it seems as if the Minutiae Monster is caught up in details, but what he is actually hung up by is the fear of making a bad decision.

A true Minutiae Monster is inherently curious. He is easily distracted by "interesting" details and has trouble staying focused on the big picture. Curiosity often leads him astray. The Minutiae Monster can spend hours researching something vaguely related to the problem at hand however tangential it is.

The Minutiae Monster is neither task-oriented nor good at setting priorities, and his work habits are poorly developed. If something strikes his fancy, he will spring into action. Too often, unfortunately, his efforts have little to do with what he is being paid to do.

What You Can Do About Minutiae Monsters

The Minutiae Monster is not hopeless. He just requires an extra measure of TLC. Break decisions down into incremental parts to address the Minutiae Monster's inability to make decisions. Realize that you can't ask the Minutiae Monster not to fixate on the details. Instead, give him micro rather than macro decisions to make. This way you're not missing the valuable observations Minutiae Monsters are capable of.

Also, don't let the Minutiae Monster languish without the tools and help necessary to get organized—start building his skills. Establishing clear priorities and deadlines for him will yield more timely responses to the demands of his job.

Focus on the little things. Consider the component parts of an issue and ask the Minutiae

Monster to give an opinion on each aspect. "This is a good overall timeline for the project," you might say. "How does this break down into daily scheduling?"

Make notes that chronicle how the Minutiae Monster's many smaller decisions and judgment calls have added up to bigger decisions with broader implications. This will diminish the Minutiae Monster's fear that making a big decision will inevitably lead to a mistake.

Reward the Minutiae Monster every time he actually does something in a reasonable amount of time. Use every opportunity to send the message that doing things in a reasonable amount of time is as important as doing them right. Remind subordinate Minutiae Monsters to balance details and output.

Build Minutiae Monsters' skill sets. Send the Minutiae Monster to formal training classes to learn time management, organization skills, and prioritizing. These should be instructor-led courses, not online classes: Self-directed lessons don't work for individuals who are prone to distraction. Make sure that the instructor understands Minutiae Monsters' issues.

Team up the Minutiae Monster with a peer mentor with strong organizational skills and efficient work habits. Such informal training will show the Minutiae Monster how good work habits will pay off and will help him learn to work better with peers.

Document the Minutiae Monster's progress in developing new skills and make note of how his behavior improves. You can then adjust the focus of the training as necessary. Your attentiveness will make the Minutiae Monster's efforts seem all the more important and consequently will reinforce them.

Set priorities. Besides their decision-making problems, obsession with detail, and poor work

---

• POWER POINTS •

LIBERATE YOUR MINUTIAE MONSTER

Minutiae Monsters can drive you crazy with details. To deal with Minutiae Monsters effectively, remember:

- Minutiae Monsters may be focusing on details to avoid work.

- Minutiae Monsters often lack organizational and time-management skills.

- Minutiae Monsters' natural curiosity can be used to your advantage— just figure out how.

- Break down large tasks into tiny ones for Minutiae Monsters.

- Provide training and peer mentoring to boost Minutiae Monsters' work skills.

- Set priorities for Minutiae Monsters that will be easy for you to monitor.

---

habits, Minutiae Monsters seem to follow every rabbit trail they come across. Sit down with the Minutiae Monster to draft a schedule that specifies priorities. Keep his focus on the task at hand by establishing what is most important to accomplish, what is second most important, and so forth. Follow through with regularly scheduled coaching sessions to monitor his progress

Outside the Box

REWARDED BEHAVIOR IS REPEATED BEHAVIOR

Rewarded behavior is behavior that will be repeated. It's a basic behavioral principle that people come forward to do things if they see a reward in it. For instance, salespeople sell more when the commission is juicy. Moreover, if people come to expect the reward and trust that it will be delivered, they repeat the actions that earned them rewards. This is why it is so important to understand what difficult people truly want. If you know what they're after, you can provide it to them; in exchange, you will enjoy behavior that is less difficult and more helpful for you and your colleagues.

SOURCE: *Communicating in Small Groups* by Steven Beebe and John Masterson (Pearson, 2003).

and note how long the Minutiae Monster stays on task. Continue to raise the bar as he improves.

Finally, recognize what the Minutiae Monster has accomplished by taking him out to lunch or publicly mentioning his contributions in the company newsletter. Use every opportunity to let the Minutiae Monster know that performance counts. You need to be directive in your leadership and peer mentoring to improve his performance. People who need more specific direction can get it through constructive confrontation—that is, written performance contracts, accountability meetings, and celebrations of progress.

THE BUSYBODY
SOMEONE WHO DOESN'T RESPECT PERSONAL AND PROFESSIONAL BOUNDARIES

Whether the Busybody is your subordinate, your coworker, or even your boss, she takes up other people's time discussing personal issues unrelated to work or gossiping about other people at work. As a coworker, the Busybody is distracting and often annoying. As a subordinate, she distracts and annoys you and your fellow team members, disrupting productivity in your department or work area. Essentially, she doesn't respect personal and professional boundaries.

What Makes the Busybody Tick?
The Busybody doesn't want to feel cut off or excluded. She has a low tolerance for solitude and is afraid to work in isolation, perceiving it as a form of social rejection. Her need for inclusion

• POWER POINTS •

REDIRECT THE BUSYBODY

People who can't seem to stay out of other people's business often don't have enough business of their own. To deal with them effectively, remember:

- Some Busybodies fear isolation; others want to be in control.

- Move the Busybody into a position that fulfills her craving for contact.

- Give the Busybody time—but direct the conversation to work issues.

- Put the Busybody to work gathering useful information for you.

- Document your dealings in case discipline is required.

can be satisfied only through interaction with other people. As she moves from one person's personal space into another's, she carries personal information about her coworkers to share. She may choose to tell these stories simply to gain acceptance—a relatively innocuous reason. But sometimes she is manipulating or trying to gain influence within the office.

What You Can Do About Busybodies

You can make the Busybody feel connected by engaging her in work-related conversations and activities. The key is to refuse to let her pull you into discussions of her personal life, your own, or that of the people around you. Take advantage of her social skills and ability to converse freely. And if that doesn't work, use your authority to put a stop to the time wasting.

Connect. Find a way to get the Busybody involved in a productive, interactive activity, such as planning employee events. Such social activities will reduce the Busybody's need to hang around her peers while they are trying to work.

Send a clear message that your time is valuable. If the Busybody is a peer, establish parameters. When the Busybody calls or shows up at your door, warn "I only have three minutes before I need to get back to this report." Delete inappropriate e-mails from the Busybody without responding.

Give Busybody bosses the time they want but direct the conversation. When you have had your fill of social banter, turn the discussion to company business. Start asking questions about work or about a meeting or presentation that you didn't attend: "Oh, by the way . . . " If your boss still wants to gab, at least it will be about official business.

Build on the Busybody's strengths. Engage the Busybody in a conversation to learn whether her curiosity about other people is genuine. Take advantage of the Busybody's seemingly constant urge to circulate among her peers in the office, gathering and disseminating information. Do you have research and information-gathering needs? If the Busybody is a subordinate, assign tasks that will draw on her natural curiosity.

Publishing a departmental newsletter? She will be your ace reporter. Need to inform team members of approaching workload issues or changing work processes? Call on the Busybody. Would she be interested in helping people

Dos & Don'ts ☑

KEEPING THE BUSYBODY BUSY

A Busybody is always interested in what is going on with her coworkers. While she may have no problems getting work done, her productivity would increase if she focused more on her own work than on what everyone on the floor was doing.

- ☐ Don't attempt to make her feel excluded.

- ☐ Do engage her in work-related discussions and occurrences.

- ☐ Do find ways to make the Busybody feel involved but at the same time productive.

- ☐ Do try and assign tasks that will utilize the Busybody's natural sense of curiosity.

- ☐ Don't let the Busybody intimidate or make others in the office feel invaded or uncomfortable.

from different departments get to know one another better and work more cooperatively? If the Busybody's interest is genuine, ask her to gather specific information from people inside or outside the company to help further your strategic and communications plans.

If the Busybody doesn't want a deeper connection with peers and does not promise to use her social skills to gather new data and information, consider the possibility that she may be trying to manipulate people. If team members report that the Busybody makes them uncomfortable and if she isn't cooperating with you, invoke your authority. Begin by starting a paper trail. Have everyone in your area regularly report in writing on the level of comfort and connectivity in the office; don't focus specifically on the Busybody, but allow the group to report on anyone and to cover any issue. If no one reports having any problems with the Busybody, you may not need to pursue further action.

If the Busybody is singled out, enforce boundaries to protect yourself—particularly if she is your boss or a peer. Gently but firmly let her know that you have limited time to spend on non-work-related conversations or activities that will delay you from getting your job done. Keep documenting. Use your best judgment. Consult your boss or someone in your human resources department if you think a problem subordinate deserves discipline or termination. At best, a Busybody is slightly annoying if sometimes amusing. At worst, a Busybody can be an enormously destructive influence, undermining your authority and diminishing the morale, productivity, and performance of the department.

THE RECLUSE

SOMEONE WHO IS ISOLATED AND DOES NOT
COMMUNICATE WITH COWORKERS

The Recluse is the person who hides in his office and avoids interaction with others. As long as he is doing his work, his isolation may not be an issue. But if his reclusive habits clog the information pipeline in your office, the Recluse becomes a problem for you as a manager trying to keep lines of communication open—and for you as a coworker who needs to interact with peers to do your job. If the Recluse is your boss, you'll be deprived of critical direction and guidance.

What Makes the Recluse Tick?

The Recluse may prefer keeping to himself for a number of reasons. He could be shy and uncomfortable around others, or a highly focused worker who doesn't like to be interrupted, or someone who has been driven into hiding by people like the Busybody. It's possible that the Recluse isolates himself because, like the Minutiae Monster, he has little experience with collaborative work and could use some training.

What You Can Do About the Recluse

Try to discern the reason for the Recluse's isolation, but don't force him to be sociable. If he's shy, find ways to interact without making him uncomfortable.

Tread lightly. Allow the Recluse to be solitary, as long as it doesn't interfere with departmental work. If you thrust him into the office social

POWER POINTS

SUPPORT A RECLUSE

Usually a very bright person with tremendous knowledge, the Recluse may fulfill an important function in your work area. For that reason, his reluctance to communicate with his colleagues is a problem. To deal with the Recluse effectively, remember:

- Understand that you will never transform your Recluse into a social butterfly.

- Stick to business in all contacts, including correspondence.

- Agree to help consolidate demands on the Recluse's time.

- Establish a routine for the Recluse to provide information to colleagues who need it.

- Keep records of the information that's exchanged between the Recluse and your staff.

- Provide appropriate skills training to the Recluse.

center, he will only barricade himself in his office in the future. If he's your subordinate, your primary interest is in the quality of his work; if he's your boss or colleague, your primary goal is to continue to have access to him and to any information you need from him.

Plan

BUILD RELATIONSHIPS WITH THIRD-PARTY COMPLIMENTS

Many difficult people behave the way they do because they feel underappreciated. Whenever you have the chance to build up a difficult person in conversation with a third party, seize the opportunity, even if he is an annoyance to you. If others say something good about him, pass on the compliment. The difficult person will appreciate hearing the comment and will feel positively toward the person who made it. Whether people do their best or worst work for someone often depends on their relationship with that person. Creating positive relationships is one way you can attempt to raise the level of someone's work. The third-party compliment technique also forces you to focus on the person's strengths rather than weaknesses.

Dos & Don'ts ☑

CLOSING IN ON THE RECLUSE

If you try to integrate a Recluse into the social network of your office or department, he will react like a fish out of water. Here are some ways to deal with a Recluse and some things that you should never do.

☐ Don't let the Recluse hinder any office communications.

☐ Do allow the Recluse to be solitary in exchange for attendance at clearly scheduled and regular meetings.

☐ Do use e-mail as a means of communication with your Recluse.

☐ Don't forget to encourage him when he does a good job, but keep the conversation from getting too personal.

☐ Do get the Recluse involved in skill-building sessions that may help him become more socially active.

☐ Don't insult your Recluse with training that is irrelevant or inappropriate for his comfort level.

You might try routinely communicating with the Recluse via e-mail, the most unsociable of all social exchanges. Keep your communication all business. If the Recluse is your subordinate, you can set up a schedule for delivering any reports or updates, paper or electronic, that may be needed to keep you and his coworkers current on his progress on joint projects.

Let the Recluse know when information he supplied accelerated the completion of a project or significantly affected the outcome in a positive way. Be succinct; there's no need to make it a social conversation. Give the good marks to the work, not the person. Be prepared to give a brief report on the same subject if you catch the Recluse out in the open, for instance, on the way to or from the restroom or elevator.

Bargain for privacy. If the Recluse is highly focused and extremely valuable, the same kind of written reporting will work. But you can also negotiate periods of guaranteed isolation in exchange for scheduled meetings that the Recluse can prepare for.

Discuss the idea of setting up a brief but regular meeting for the Recluse and your team. Have questions and information requests submitted in advance, if possible. In return, you will promise to secure his work time and consolidate information requests.

If you manage a department or a work area, limit others' access to Recluse. If he is bombarded with requests for information, nobody will get what they want. If you coordinate the flow, everybody will benefit. If the Recluse is your boss, don't bother him with details and minutiae. Find out what is most important to him and use his need for that kind of information to gain access.

Invest in training. Like the Minutiae Monster, the Recluse may be the way he is in part because of a lack of skills. If this is the case, you can get the Recluse involved in peer mentoring or hire an outside trainer. Concentrate on building communication skills and educating him about interpersonal dynamics.

Make sure the training is relevant to your needs. Many organizations send people to training where business issues of all kinds are painted with a broad brush. Your Recluse may have a superior intellect and be a valued member of your team, so don't insult him with inappropriate or irrelevant training. Talk to the Recluse before sending him for training and explain what you expect and why.

THE BULLY
SOMEONE WHO DELIBERATELY
INTIMIDATES OTHERS

Bullies pose a problem at work whether they're subordinates, colleagues, or bosses. A Bully who works for you may steer clear of your authority but take advantage of your other team members. Your team members will look to you to protect them, so you wind up battling the Bully anyway. If the Bully is your peer, you have just as much of a problem on your hands but little or no authority to deal with it. If the Bully is your boss, you're vulnerable.

What Makes a Bully Tick?

Although your typical Bully looks and sounds fierce, she is often hurting. Neatly summing up the practice of bullying, a 10-year-old prep school boy once told British philosopher Bertrand Russell, "The bigs hit me, so I hit the smalls. That's fair." Ultimately, Bully's goal is to feel "big"—that is, important or worthwhile. In her own strange way, Bully is really asking you to be her friend and to show her respect and acceptance. But she is her own worst enemy, making enemies along the way.

What You Can Do About the Bully

You can either befriend the Bully or focus her energy on other activities. If the Bully is your subordinate, your challenge is to find a way to use your authority to prevent the Bully from

---

Behind the Numbers

BOSSES WHO BULLY

According to Bennett Tepper, a professor of managerial sciences at Georgia State University in Atlanta, studies show that 10 to 16 percent of employees are bullied by their supervisors. And an outstanding 50 percent of employees report having worked for an abusive manager during their career.

SOURCES: "Three Tips for Coping with a Nightmare Boss" by Andrea Coombes, *Marketwatch* (July 20, 2006).

---

picking on your other subordinates. The worst use of your authority is to bully her, which might prompt her to abuse weaker and less aggressive people. Your authority is better used to help the Bully find alternative behaviors. It is within your

• POWER POINTS •

DON'T TAKE THE BULLY'S BAIT
Bullying a bully consumes energy and may not work. To more effectively deal with a Bully, remember:

- A Bully covers up insecurities by puffing herself up.

- Often the Bully is behaving just as others did toward her as a child.

- Bullies thrive on fear; if you're intimidated, don't show it.

- Try to understand what makes the Bully feel inadequate.

- Keep your cool.

- Engage the Bully with sincere curiosity about her work.

- Note what you're told so that you can follow up later.

- Over-deliver to a Bully boss and give her credit for the things she does as a boss.

capacity to alter—dramatically—the behavior of this difficult person.

Divert the Bully's energy elsewhere. Observe the Bully's work to determine her skills. What type of work suits her best? What special training has the Bully received? What are her strengths? Hold constructive conversations with her; probe to figure out what she values about work and what kind of recognition she needs. Don't focus on the bad behavior. Instead, without asking in so many words, you want to find out what will make her feel important.

Use your authority to give the Bully additional, high-visibility responsibility in an area where she can excel. Make the assignment conditional and probationary but a real expression of your confidence. Set Bully up to win by assigning her to projects with others that use Bully's competencies and result in her strengths being recognized. Be patient as Bully tries to adjust.

Befriend your Bully peer or boss. If you're being bullied by a peer, don't let the Bully sense that she has successfully intimidated you. Similarly, don't try and bully back. By her nature, the Bully tries to prove herself strongest, so if you escalate the conflict, you're only inviting disaster. Appealing to your boss might prove fruitless. In short, to stop the aggression, you need to befriend the Bully.

To win the Bully over, take a special interest in her work. Be patient; Bullies are not used to people taking an active interest in their life and work. Ask specific questions that you know she will be able to answer about work. Follow her lead.

Dos & Don'ts ☑

DON'T BE BULLIED BY A BULLY

Don't let Bullies be a driving force of intimidation in your workplace. When dealing with Bullies, follow these tips.

☐ Do help the Bully find other, non-threatening behaviors to deal with her insecurities.

☐ Don't focus on bad behavior, but rather focus on what might make the Bully feel more important or valued as a worker.

☐ Do set the Bully up to win by putting her in a situation where her skills will be recognized and her performance successful.

☐ Don't forget to take a special interest in her work and other interests.

☐ Don't let a Bully-boss bully you. Whatever you do, overdo it, and give your boss 110 percent.

☐ Don't give a bully the satisfaction of knowing she has successfully intimidated you.

Don't give advice about future actions. Instead, talk about current projects, and ask her how she would like her responsibilities to grow.

If the Bully is your boss, there is no question of fighting back. You are powerless. You can seek help from human resources or others at or above your boss's level of authority, but if your boss is successful or popular, your best approach is to draw on the techniques you would use for a Bully peer. You will become a more skilled communicator in the process.

Respond to your boss's orders like any dutiful employee; you don't want to set yourself up as being insubordinate. Remember your work assignments and confirm them in an e-mail to create a virtual paper trail. Then over-deliver. Keep your work beyond reproach and give your Bully-boss every reason to believe that you care about her success. But don't respond to bullying tactics. Instead, make special note of what's important to your boss. Are there sports trophies in her office? Pictures? Or anything else that would indicate a special interest of some kind? Take a special interest in what your boss does and how well she does it. Don't be put off by peers accusing you of kissing up. You're executing a proven technique for surviving an abusive boss. When she starts feeling appreciated and important, she will stop bullying you and your peers—something for which they will thank you.

THE LIAR

A PERSON WHO DELIBERATELY BREAKS THE
RULES AND MISLEADS YOU

Dishonesty is a tough thing to deal with in the workplace, and dishonest people are among the most difficult. Dishonesty causes difficulty on several levels. Among the ranks of honest, rule-abiding employees, the Liar is the lowest on the credibility list. But right next to the Liar is a boss who engages in denial, is too timid to act, or

CASE *FILE*

THINK AHEAD WHEN YOU BLOW THE WHISTLE

Sherron Watkins, former vice president of corporate development for Enron, is credited with blowing the whistle on the corporate corruption within her company and at accounting firm Arthur Andersen. Although she was not fired in retaliation, she became an outcast, according to Frank Pellegrini, writing in *Time* magazine. In another case, in which there was no public scrutiny and litigation is pending, a manager in a Silicon Valley software company who exposed overspending when less expensive competitive bids were available was demoted after reporting the news to his boss. The company's reason: He was a "difficult person to work with." Be careful when you try to "out" a Liar.

SOURCE: "Issues Management, Systems, and Rhetoric" by Shannon A. Bowen and Robert L. Heath, *Journal of Public Affairs* (August 25, 2005).

enables a Liar. If the Liar is a peer, the pressure to do something can still be high because you need to avoid guilt by association. If the Liar is your own boss, you have yet another set of issues: The threat of guilt by association is still there, but the possibility of being implicated without your knowledge is much greater.

What Makes a Liar Tick?

This person has an ethical problem. Sometimes Liars fall into unethical behavior because it's the easiest way to get what they want; they seem to get away with it, so they think, "Why not?" Perhaps the Liar was brought up in the business world by unscrupulous people and doesn't know any other way to operate. Or perhaps the Liar believes that outfoxing someone else makes him smart. Some people believe that the ability to get something out of someone else by questionable means is the very essence of power.

What You Can Do About a Liar

Depending on how quickly and effectively you deal with the situation and how well your solutions resonate with your boss's ideas, your job could be at stake. The first thing to do is to weigh your options. Then take action—decisive and possibly defensive action.

Take decisive action. Dealing with a Liar is a challenge, but the sooner you take action, the better. As soon as you feel something fishy is happening, start documenting it. Keeping records heads off the problems that fuzzy or selective memory can cause later on.

If your knowledge of the situation is stronger than a mere hunch or unsubstantiated accusation from another subordinate, get your boss involved. Explain that you're documenting the situation and preparing to confront the Liar. Tell your boss you want the guidance of someone in human resources.

• POWER POINTS •

TREAD GENTLY AROUND A LIAR

Liars are tricky to deal with—you never know where you stand. Your Liar might be trying to usurp your authority, steal your job, or just get away with something you wouldn't condone. To deal most effectively with a Liar, remember:

- Being honest yourself will not convert a Liar. Don't let yourself be exploited.

- Take defensive action if the Liar is your coworker.

- Make sure your boss isn't in on the lie before going to her for help.

- Document your case against the Liar so that it's not your opinion versus his.

- Use your human resources department to back you up with its authority and procedures.

Appeal to the Liar's need to feel powerful. With your boss's blessing, give the Liar more power in your department. It's a risky move but could diminish the Liar's urge to be unethical. Make the new position conditional and probationary.

Take defensive action. If the Liar is your coworker, don't get caught up in whatever is going on. If you yourself manage to steer clear, you still face the ethical dilemma of whether or not to expose the situation. This is a complex problem because doing the right thing may not produce the outcome you want. In business, it often happens that people report up the chain of command as dictated by company policy—only to find themselves ostracized or worse because of their actions. To avoid this situation, document

Dos & Don'ts ☑

WORKING WITH A LIAR

It is difficult to work with a Liar because of the erosion of a sense of trust. Liars have a tendency to be evasive and with-hold important information from you, as well as telling outright lies. In dealing with a Liar, remember the following tips.

- ☐ Do keep excellent records of your suspicions as they arise.
- ☐ Don't get yourself into trouble; you want to avoid becoming a target of blame or wrongdoing.

what you have observed, including times, dates,
people, and places; leave none of this to memory.
Down the road, you may need to prove how you
found out about the Liar's activities and how
your knowledge expanded. The written record
could help clear your name if you are accused of
complicity.

Evaluate the scope of the problem. It is not
uncommon for unethical behavior to spread.
Be aware that your boss could be aware of the
situation and turning a blind eye or even par-
ticipating. If you can, find out if this is the case
before you ask for help. If that's not the case,
ask your boss's permission to involve human
resources. Then follow human resource's recommendations, even if you think you have a

☐ Do get your boss involved if the Liar
is a peer or subordinate. If necessary,
contact human resources and file a
complaint with them as well.

☐ Do appeal to the Liar's need to exert
his power.

☐ Do try and diminish the Liar's tendency to be unethical and dishonest.

☐ Do think about what risks are involved
in trying to expose the Liar.

better plan. Remember that you are trying to clear the air so that you can get back to work. Weigh your options carefully.

Some Liars are beyond your control because they are above you on the organization chart, people you report to directly, or in an unrelated area of the company. You should think long and hard about what you're willing to risk in dealing with them. If you do want to take the high road, keep good records of what you suspect is going on. By documenting details, you show arbitrators that you have been seeking the truth. Stick to the facts, and don't add conjecture or conspiracy theories. E-mails, memos, and official records and documents speak a lot louder than unsubstantiated speculation.

Discuss your next step with your family or someone outside the organization. You might be advised to let sleeping dogs lie; exposing a lie or breach of integrity may not be worth your job. However, if you are implicated by association or if you are the one being swindled, you need to do something, and the accuracy of your documentation will make a huge difference. If and when Liars are implicated, don't be surprised if false accusations start flying in your direction.

Be ready with Plan B. If the Liar has authority over you, go straight to human resources for help before confronting him. Then be prepared for the backlash. Human resources needs to give the Liar a fair hearing. Be prepared to be shunned, as whistle-blowers often are. Expect to be targeted by the Liar's peers for ratting out their comrade.

Once you confront the situation, no matter how good your documentation or how strong the promises of support from human resources, there may be consequences. Be prepared.

Whether the Liar is a subordinate, peer, or superior, you must weigh the pros and cons of doing something or letting it go.

THE OUTLAW
SOMEONE WHO DOESN'T PLAY BY THE RULES UNLESS THEY'RE HIS OWN

An Outlaw has never met a rule or regulation she likes. In the belief that everybody should be free to come and go as they like, she defies convention. Sometimes the outlaw becomes a folk hero—or at the very least, an unfortunate role model. For that reason, if an Outlaw is not dealt with effectively in your department, she might inspire team members to follow her lead. Because of the disorganizing effect an Outlaw can have on your staff, she is difficult to work with, especially as your subordinate.

What Makes the Outlaw Tick?
Outlaws feel trapped, bound, and constrained by rules. Some go about their business, doing their jobs without causing problems and ignoring rules only when they get in the way.

Some Outlaws are okay with rules that everyone else obeys as long as they are an exception. For these Outlaws, it's all about not being like everybody else. More fanatical Outlaws, the true iconoclasts, resist conformity or compliance with regulations on principle. They seem compelled to challenge authority. Many are frustrated by a lack of success when they play by conventional methods, or they feel they're not achieving what they deserve—and they blame the rules.

What You Can Do About Outlaws

Ignoring the rules is not always bad. You can learn a lesson from the Outlaws working for you: Questioning authority and the way things have always been done can give you some new ideas. Nurture curiosity among your staff. Loosen the reins a bit.

Focus on creativity, not compliance. Ask the Outlaw to tell you which policies she finds

Dos & Don'ts ☑

LAYING DOWN THE LAW WITH AN OUTLAW

You may feel that Outlaws are always stirring up trouble in the office. They may feel that it is their personal mission to rearrange office politics, while most of the time they do nothing but give you grief about your business practices.

☐ Do invite the Outlaw to tell you which rules and policies bother her most and why.

☐ Do schedule a department-wide discussion of policies and rules that may need updating or overhauling.

the most cumbersome and unproductive. Ask "Why? How exactly do these rules reduce personal performance and departmental productivity?" Write down her answers. Chances are that old ways of doing things have been hampering others as well.

Set up a time to challenge rules on a regular basis. That way, the Outlaw will have a forum in which to express her dislike of rules—but a forum that you control. If you do get rid of rules that are unnecessary and cumbersome, explain why in a memo to all employees and attribute the idea to the Outlaw who helped you. Receiving recognition as "rule busters" is very important to Outlaws.

- [ ] Don't neglect to stress the end results that the department needs to achieve and try to streamline all discussions and activities to meet these goals.
- [ ] Do assign the Outlaw a position on a "Rules and Results Team," which will put her partially in charge of seeing that new rules and regulations are enforced and relevant.
- [ ] Do award prizes to people for things such as "best suggestion" or to those whose ideas gather the most support from other employees.

Outside the Box

ORGANIZE FOR CREATIVITY

Many people fall into lockstep behind an organizational rebel contending that rules stifle creativity. They believe that organization of any kind smothers the creative spark and makes spontaneity impossible. According to Mike Vance and Diane Deacon, coauthors of *Think Out of the Box,* procedures and policies are actually important to open up space so that people can create. According to Deacon and Vance, it's the uncontrolled environment that undermines creativity. When there is no structure, people have to figure out for themselves what they're supposed to be doing. If someone comes up with a radical idea or solution in a disorganized or chaotic environment, it's often a result of luck. Creativity will flourish in an organized environment.

SOURCE: *Think Out of the Box* by Diane Deacon and Mike Vance (Career Press, 1995).

Make challenging the rules a department-wide event. Give every wannabe Outlaw a chance to be defiant. Use the energy and momentum that rebels in the organization are capable of generating to your advantage by getting people excited about remaking existing policies. In effect, you are using your employees' rebellious streak to have them come up with ways to manage better.

Start with a town hall meeting. Have some fun with it. Your ultimate goal is to suggest new

• POWER POINTS •

THE OUTLAW

An Outlaw's mystique appeals to the rebel in everyone. The more popular the Outlaw, the more difficult she is to those who are accountable for productivity and performance. To deal effectively with Outlaws, remember:

- Be forewarned that adopting a "rules for rules' sake" position won't counteract the Outlaw's influence.

- Enlist the Outlaw's help in stream-lining your systems. She is good at recognizing procedures and rules that have outlived their usefulness.

- Push creativity over compliance.

- Hold town hall meetings to empha-size your openness to suggestions.

- Create a rules-bashing team that includes the Outlaw.

policies and procedures to enhance the performance and productivity of your department or work area. Review existing protocols and then open the floor for discussion. Demonstrate to the Outlaw that neither you nor her coworkers are hidebound and that everything is subject to discussion.

Challenge team members to suggest alternative policies and procedures that will help them do a better job reaching departmental goals. Give prizes for the best suggestions or those that receive the most support. Write up the meeting

CASE *FILE*

TAKE THE TIME TO ENGINEER TRANSFORMATION

Investing the time to hear what's troubling a difficult employee can turn around a situation. Mary Mayhre, director of organizational transformation for CIBER, an international systems integration consulting firm, was working with a small company as it implemented new human resources software.

Tammy, a human resources employee, was unhappy because the new software would significantly change her job. Employees had relied upon Tammy to create reports for them, but with the new system, employees would be able to create their own reports.

ideas as an action proposal that is endorsed by the Outlaw herself. Point out that this document reflects the consensus of town hall participants. Your people have told you how they think things should be run and you're ready to use your authority to carry it out.

Create a new order. You want your entire staff to feel as if they can operate outside the box. There's nothing wrong with that. But your department's activities are governed by your company's overarching goals, and your department's procedures and rules must reflect that. That's how you complete the circle you've created by indulging the Outlaw. Tie all discussion

Anticipating the change, Tammy became abrupt and uncooperative. Mayhre spoke with Tammy, telling her that she would still be very important to the department because of her technical skills and her understanding of the new software. Mary pointed out to Tammy that people would come to her with questions whenever they were having problems with the software and were frustrated.

As a result of this conversation, Tammy became the company's go-to person to deal with the system. Tammy also became more engaged and more helpful. All it took was someone to remind Tammy how important she was to the people around her.

and activities to the results and outcomes your department needs to achieve.

Create "Rules and Results Teams" to review how policies are enhancing or impeding your work processes. This lets the Outlaw know that she doesn't have exclusive claim to challenging the status quo. But make sure you implement new systems and work processes that the Rules and Results Team recommends. If you don't act on suggestions, team members will feel that their contributions are merely window dressing and the positive benefits will be lost.

Place the Outlaw in charge of maintaining order by including her on the Rules and Results Team. This makes her directly responsible for enforcing rules. That's a paradoxical bind. But if you have set up the overall goals and outcomes of the department as targets to be hit, the Outlaw has to figure out how to make it happen. She may surprise you with the sense of responsibility she demonstrates when placed in a position of authority.

THE BLAMER-COMPLAINER
SOMEONE WHO BLAMES YOU AND OTHERS
FOR HIS MISTAKES

Sometimes called Whiners because of their tone of voice when blaming and complaining, Blamer-Complainers are probably the most common type of difficult people. Their tone of voice alone makes them difficult to work with. Equally irritating is how they pass the buck, find fault in everyone and everything,

Dos & Don'ts ☑

THE BLAMER-COMPLAINER

When you have a Blamer-Complainer working in your department, you have your hands full. Usually this type of person is terrified of being held accountable when he makes an error on the job.

☐ Don't forget to accept blame when you make a mistake. This is crucial to demonstrate the necessity of shared responsibility.

☐ Do place the Blamer-Complainer in teams with like-minded individuals and stress that teamwork requires shared responsibilities, and therefore shared blame.

☐ Do eliminate blaming and complaining and replace them with constructive and action-oriented problem solving.

☐ Don't overlook a Blamer-Complainer when you need someone with a critical eye to assess a project that is going wrong.

☐ Don't forget to be tactful when disputing wrongful blame if your boss is a Blamer-Complainer.

and enroll other people in their poor decisions. Blamer-Complainers are a drain on morale and esprit de corps.

What Makes the Blamer-Complainer Tick?

Blamer-Complainers can't stand the thought of being wrong. They are intolerant of imperfection, whether in themselves or others. No matter what happens and no matter where the smoking gun is found, it's never the Blamer–Complainer's fault.

Blamer-Complainers don't accept that being human sometimes means making mistakes. They are seemingly incapable of adopting the "forgive, learn, and move on" attitude. They can't accept that their thinking might be flawed, which is why they start pointing at you. Blamer-Complainers, like Bullies, are most aggressive with their most vulnerable targets.

What You Can Do About the Blamer-Complainer

If the Blamer-Complainer works for you or is a peer, you will probably not be able to convince him to accept responsibility for failure; instead, preempt him by adopting a shared-responsibility policy. Set a fine example, accepting blame for mistakes when you make them.

Spread out the responsibility. Make the tactical move to put the Blamer-Complainer on a team with like-minded people. Teamwork requires everyone to share responsibility for planning and executing a project, including addressing any problems that may arise. In a team situation, the Blamer-Complainer will be subject to peer pressure to share accountability. Coach the team to adopt shared responsibility going into projects, not merely after things go wrong.

• POWER POINTS •

THE BLAMER-COMPLAINER

A Blamer-Complainer rains on anybody's parade. Your best bet is to anticipate the sour attitude, set up a positive atmosphere, and look for the strengths in everything and everyone. To deal effectively with Blamer-Complainers, remember:

- Anticipate the possibility that mistakes will be made and talk about it upfront.

- Spread out responsibility across teams so no one person is vulnerable to blame.

- Accept blame when you deserve it.

- Be humble, especially with a Blamer-Complainer boss.

- Heap on the praise to make the Blamer-Complainer feel important.

- Cover yourself—document what you've done in case the Blamer-Complainer targets you.

The acknowledgment that there will be mistakes, miscues, misfires, and miscalculations will help everyone accept responsibility for snafus, including the Blamer-Complainer.

Acknowledge the good and the bad. Every team that makes mistakes does a lot of things right, too. The things that are done well deserve as much discussion and documentation as the things that went wrong—and at equal, if not greater, volume. Helping teammates chronicle recommendations for future projects will shift the Blamer-Complainer's focus in a positive direction.

CASE FILE

WORSE THAN THE DISEASE

Betty was a competent financial director, but she also monitored everyone's work habits and commented whenever she saw lapses. Her peers at Tape Data Media felt indignant and insulted by this coworker, who presumed some sort of moral authority over them. Operating outside of her institutional authority, Betty caused a tremendous amount of animosity and friction around the office. So the department manager sought to deal swiftly with the problem; unfortunately, he didn't think through how he could handle the problem most effectively.

Instead, he decided to give Betty a chance to explain why she engaged in

Set the example. Bosses goof up just like anyone else, and it builds employees' spirits to hear a boss admit a mistake. Show subordinates, especially the Blamer-Complainer, that it's okay to make a mistake. Encourage people to think carefully about what went wrong. For example, say "We made progress toward getting the outcomes we're looking for. Now let's take a hard look at the lessons we learned this time around and how we can improve next time."

Campaign against fault-finding. Acknowledge that people make mistakes, but reward people who offer solutions by giving them extra time off or the problem-solver-of-the-month parking

this behavior at a meeting with the most interested parties. Betty was given the floor first and explained why she felt misunderstood and isolated. She produced statistics she had compiled to demonstrate how much harder she worked than anyone else. Her colleagues were nervous and uncomfortable, too stunned to say anything. At the end of the meeting, nothing was resolved.

As lawyers often say, never ask a question you don't know the answer to. Betty's manager learned that he shouldn't have called a general meeting about a problem unless he was fully prepared for what might happen.

SOURCE: *How to Work for an Idiot* by John Hoover (Career Press, 2003).

space—whatever is appropriate—while ignoring those who blame and complain. Recognizing and encouraging problem solvers will give Blamer–Complainers motivation to change.

Correct correspondence. Don't stop at eliminating the use of blaming and complaining terminology in conversation; make sure it doesn't creep into written communications and documents. If the Blamer-Complainer has a tendency to point out blame in his e-mails, letters, or other documents, call him on it. Encourage people to use positive, solution-oriented language. Say to them, "Instead of telling me who is to blame, give me solutions and better practices to follow."

Cover your backside. If your boss is the Blamer-Complainer, your only option is to keep meticulous records of your work so that he cannot complain about your work or blame you.

Be humble. Don't argue with your Blamer-Complainer boss if he has the least bit of evidence that you have not performed as well as could be expected. Take the information your boss provides and write up guidelines you will follow to improve your performance next time. Then get the Blamer-Complainer to sign off on this "contract" in writing. Follow your new guidelines, then send him a report of your work, complete with the initial "contract." Your Blamer-Complainer boss might not find anything positive about your performance, but he won't be able to find fault with it either.

If you document your achievements, when the opportunity arises to apply for another job, you will have a good track record to boast about. Your Blamer-Complainer boss cannot legally say bad things to a prospective new employer. As much as he loves to blame and complain, confirming the legitimacy of paperwork he signed off on is about the only action available to your former Blamer-Complainer boss.

Whereas Blamer-Complainers can be irritating, they can also be helpful. When you need a critical eye to look at a project and tell you what's going wrong, the Blamer-Complainer may well be your best consultant. Want to find the potential problems with a proposal? Pitch it to a Blamer-Complainer. What he gripes about could help you save money, time, and effort later on.

THE KNOW-IT-ALL

SOMEONE WHO CLAIMS TO KNOW EVERY-
THING ABOUT EVERYTHING

A Know-It-All can disrupt your operation from top to bottom. Wanting to be in control, this type of difficult person pays little attention to what others say. She is condescending and irritating. Unlike the Recluse, who keeps his opinions to himself, the Know-It-All is quick to share opinions. If your boss is a Know-It-All, the condescension is especially irritating. Managing a Know-It-All is equally difficult; she readily defies your authority and insults your staff, annoying and alienating coworkers. Because of the Know-It-All's behavior, people don't like her, and her contribution is not what it could be, given her intelligence.

What Makes the Know-It-All Tick?

The illusion of superior intelligence anchors the Know-It-All's self-esteem. While she might indeed be very smart, what matters to her is to be perceived as the smartest of all. The need to

POWER POINT

THE KNOW-IT-ALL

One of the reasons Know-It-Alls are particularly difficult is that they often are the brightest bulb in the box. To deal most effectively with the Know-It-All, remember:

• Know-It-Alls defy your intellectual authority.

• Take contempt in stride, consider the source, and use Know-It-Alls' desire to dispense information in your favor. Let them educate you and your staff.

• Give your Know-It-All credit for knowing important information.

• Get your Know-It-All involved in research and data gathering.

• Encourage others to use the Know-It-All as a resource.

• Share the Know-It-All with other departments.

be valued for her intellect often compensates for poor self-esteem and, in some cases, for a lack of knowledge.

To ensure her place at the top of the intellectual pecking order, the Know-It-All tries to control everything she is involved with. That way, if she lacks certain information or knowledge, she has the power to cover it up. The Know-It-All is rarely the most athletically gifted or socially magnetic person in the department. It is the brainpower they boast about that is the source of their pride.

What You Can Do About the Know-It-All

There is little that can be done to change a person's self-image. However, you can organize your department to accommodate the Know-It-All and give her a chance to participate and be recognized for what she does know. If the Know-It-All is your peer, you can also play to her strengths rather than become an antagonist. To start with, don't challenge her intellectual superiority. This is especially important if the Know-It-All is your boss or someone higher. You'll just make an enemy you don't need.

Let the Know-It-All be the smartest of the smart. Graciously accept the information she shares. You never know when information, no matter how abrasive the source, might be helpful.

Encourage the Know-It-All to participate. Go to the Know-It-All for information first. Ask for her help figuring something out. When research needs to be done, assign it to the Know-It-All, and get her involved in departmental activities

Dos & Don'ts ☑

BEFRIEND THE KNOW-IT-ALL

A Know-It-All is very intelligent and may even know more about the company than you do. She is usually very informed and always chimes in with her opinions. It's important that you make the Know-It-All feel that her wealth of information is of value to you and your company.

☐ Don't challenge the Know-It-All's intelligence, but rather give her projects and tasks that take advantage of her wealth of information.

☐ Do encourage the Know-It-All to participate by going to her first with questions that she can answer. Compliment her on her knowledge.

☐ Do assign leadership positions to the Know-It-All on information-gathering projects and activities.

☐ Do share the Know-It-all with other departments and involve her at interdepartmental meetings where she can gain exposure to other areas of the company.

☐ Don't forget to praise the Know-It-All often, which will build her self-esteem and confirm that she is a valued member of the team.

that play well into her self-image. Compliment and reward her for having vital knowledge that you need. Businesses run on information. The Know-It-All is a valuable asset.

Challenge the Know-It-All to go deeper. It's one thing to know facts and figures. If the Know-It-All is conducting research on your behalf or for the team you're on, ask how her findings can best be applied. Then put her opinion to highly visible use.

Make practical assignments. Putting the Know-It-All in charge of solving complex puzzles makes sense, given her strong desire to know everything. Gathering contact data for a marketing campaign that includes studying demographics, geographical release timing, product planning, and preparation will really draw on the Know-It-All's brainpower.

Give the Know-It-All team leadership responsibility for information-related activities. Choose other people who are also curious and research-oriented to be part of the team. They will appreciate the Know-It-All's desire for knowledge. Make the team assignment clear. Tell them: "We need information that we can use right now to extend our competitive advantage. So-and-so here is an expert at gathering and analyzing data. All of you can participate and, together, you can turn the raw data into useful information."

Share your Know-It-All. Tell other department heads and your boss that, if you had a position for a Chief Knowledge Officer, your Know-It-All would have the title. It won't hurt your career ambitions or standing within the organization to be a champion of applied knowledge. Or ask the Know-It-All to join you at high-level meetings to advise on data resource issues. Instead of playing the role of "font of all information," defer to the Know-It-All. When acknowledged, she won't feel a need to convince others of the superiority of her intellect.

> "People of character do the hard work first. Then, as a result, they are ready for things to be easy for a long time."
>
> Dr. Henry Cloud,
> author of *Integrity*

Ask the Know-It-All to represent you and the department at interdepartmental meetings. Tell her you have faith in her knowledge of the department. She will be able to represent the department well and answer all questions, especially the detailed questions that demand an explanation of the thinking behind decisions. Ask the Know-It-All to begin creating an information warehouse to document all of the information and resources important to your department. This plays into the Know-It-All's natural desire to be Information Central. Demand that the information warehouse be accessible to everyone who can put the data to good use.

The more you acknowledge the Know-It-All's intelligence, the less contempt she will express toward you and others. Give credit where credit is due. The more you pump up and publicize the Know-It-All's good work, the less she will want to be put in charge of everything else, too. Even with Know-It-Alls, rewarded behavior is repeated behavior.

BE PREPARED FOR ANYTHING

You now have a better idea of the many ways people can be difficult to work with and why. Note that not all difficult people will fit neatly into the ten categories described above. Also, be aware that you'll encounter difficult people who will behave in the most unconventional and unpredictable ways imaginable—intentionally or not. Be ready for anything. In any event, always be prepared to act decisively. Not dealing with difficult people is a concession that you will allow the sabotage of your ability to manage effectively.

HOW TO HANDLE DIFFICULT PEOPLE

"Your goal [is to] make your bosses smarter, your team more effective, and the whole company more competitive because of your energy, creativity, and insights."

—Jack Welch

To be an asset to your company, you need to be a problem solver. In other words, you need to be skilled at making problems go away. To manage all difficult people and the problems that come with them, you need to remember one basic principle: First, you must separate the problem from the person.

Self-Assessment Quiz

YOUR WORK STYLE

Just as everyone's personality is different, ways of dealing with various office situations vary from person to person. Answer the following questions as honestly as possible, thinking only about how you behave in the situations described, not how you think you should behave.

1. When an elevator is crowded I
   [A] shove my way in
   [B] shove my way in only if I'm in a huge hurry
   [C] step back and wait for the next elevator, worrying about the time I'm wasting.

2. When I have something I want to say in a meeting I
   [A] speak up freely
   [B] raise my hand and request permission to speak
   [C] speak only when spoken to or else keep my opinions to myself.

3. When I encounter a conversation among my peers in the hallway I
   [A] jump in regardless of the topic
   [B] stop and listen from the perimeter
   [C] don't stop to listen.

4. When I walk past my boss's office I
   [A] make it a point to say hello
   [B] wave only if he waves first

[C] avoid meeting my boss's eyes.

5. When my boss stops by my workspace I
   [A] greet him warmly and immediately engage in work talk
   [B] say, "Yes?" (i.e., "What are you here for?") and answer only the specific questions he asks
   [C] duck out of my cubicle and hide in the restroom

6. When a subordinate wants me to explain something to her I
   [A] seize the opportunity to hold a mini-seminar and make it a quality teaching moment
   [B] give her the best information I have or suggest who else might know
   [C] duck out of my office and hide around the corner until the coast is clear.

7. When my boss wants me to explain something that happened I
   [A] seize the opportunity to pitch new ideas and recount my latest triumphs
   [B] give my boss a brief but thorough answer or suggest who else might know
   [C] call in sick.

Self-Assessment Quiz

8. When someone at work steals my ideas and presents them as her own, I

   [A] confront the person and let the boss know that the ideas originated with me

   [B] determine whether or not my co-worker's plagiarism is costing me anything and make a plan to get some recognition if it's important enough

   [C] roll over, forget that idea, and hope my boss comes in and asks me directly for my ideas next time.

9. When someone at work irritates me by harassing me and ordering me around, I

   [A] get in his face and put an end to the behavior

   [B] find a credible reason for doing all or some of what he is demanding so I won't feel like a doormat

   [C] do what I'm told because I don't want to risk a confrontation.

10. When someone at work hangs around my workspace and follows me everywhere, including the restroom, I

   [A] tell that person to get out of my space and threaten consequences if she doesn't

   [B] accommodate the person up to a

point and then excuse myself to
work

[C] take the person under my wing and
give her the time and attention she
wants, even if my own work suffers.

Scoring

Give yourself 2 points for every A answer,
1 point for every B answer, and 0 points for
every C answer.

Analysis

15–20   Assertive type. You deal with
matters assertively and with
confidence and expect to be
effective. You are often the leader
of your work team, softball team,
or ad hoc committee.

8–14   Collaborative type. You are less
aggressive but take your responsibilities seriously. You serve as
the group leader, but you seek the
involvement of others.

1–7   Passive type. You'd really rather
not deal with anyone unless you
have to. You do not like being
asked to do anything outside of
your comfort zone. Rather than
leading, you prefer to be out of
the line of fire, where you can get
your work done.

If you are able to react to the personality and in the process preserve your relationship with the person whenever possible, you'll eliminate the problem altogether.

WHY NOT JUST FIRE THE PERSON?

Without question, one obvious solution to dealing with a difficult person is to get rid of him. But that is not always easy, even if the person is your subordinate. Having institutional power over someone does not give you unlimited rights to terminate his employment, even if that is the best option. Moreover, terminating an employee can be a complex legal process.

The cost of replacing a person is another reason to try to salvage the relationship first. The person may have talent and knowledge that are valuable to the company. If the informal strategies described in chapter two have not been effective, it's preferable to explore more formalized ways to solve the problem. Especially if you are dealing with a difficult subordinate, you have choices you can make before you set the wheels in motion for termination. Perhaps the most powerful of these choices is to confront the need for increased accountability and diminished conflict sooner rather than later.

THE ART OF CONSTRUCTIVE CONFRONTATION

One of the best of these coping skills, and a valuable alternative to termination, is *constructive confrontation,* a structured cycle of discussion; commitment and covenant; scheduled feedback sessions; and celebration. Each of these elements has been used in the workplace for decades and produced tremendous results in leadership, team, and individual performance. Constructive conversations are a staple of conflict resolution, conflict prevention, and coalition building.

The BIG Picture

DIFFICULT PEOPLE SLOW DOWN CHANGE

Change is hard enough to make happen even when everyone is cooperative. One of the reasons you may need to terminate a difficult person is that change throughout an organization requires as many supporters as possible. In fact, according to John P. Kotter, it takes the cooperation of 15 to 25 percent of employees to produce significant results. But often difficult people are like big rocks blocking the path to change. They can undermine your ability to win the hearts and minds of the 15 to 25 percent of employees you'll need to charge up the hill. If difficult people are indeed getting in the way of much needed change in your organization, consider termination.

SOURCE: *Leading Change* by John P. Kotter (Harvard Business School Press, 1996).

Covenants, or personal contracts, have long been used in business to increase accountability and guide performance, especially for salespeople. Feedback sessions are indispensable to good management. Celebration is simply the formal recognition of employees' progress, whether in their attitude, performance, or work habits.

THE CONSTRUCTIVE CONFRONTATION CYCLE

The combination of these four proven elements together is powerful. There are no better techniques to fully engage employees and deal effectively with difficult people in the workplace.

Constructive confrontation can be used to address miscommunication between managers and their direct reports. It can solve many of the problems that occur between coworkers and the difficulties you may be having with your boss. With constructive confrontation, problems are addressed sooner, while they are small and manageable, rather than later, when they've grown so large and unwieldy that any attempt to address them will probably be negative. Dealing with problem behaviors early and repeatedly gives you the most leverage to keep them under control. The natural results of constructive confrontation are increased accountability and reduced conflict between bosses and subordinates.

Step One: Conversation

The cycle of constructive confrontation begins with a conversation. When an employee is being difficult, engage her in a conversation, preferably in her work space. Bringing a subordinate into your office might intimidate her and prevent her from opening up to you.

In discussing whatever behavioral issues there might be, also talk about her job responsibilities and how they are to be carried out. Purposely keep the conversation positive by asking for your subordinate's point of view. How does she perceive her role in the department? What are her expectations of her subordinates, of her colleagues, and of you, her manager? Are her

Outside the Box

CONFRONTATION AS PROBLEM SOLVING

The best advice for leaders, according to author and psychologist Henry Cloud, is his friend's policy: "I go hard on the issue and soft on the person." In other words, when you need to confront a staff member, bring to the table both your high work expectations and standards and a sympathetic ear. Focus on what you want to get out of the confrontation. You should approach it as an opportunity for problem solving. As Dr. Cloud explains: "To solve the problem, make the relationship stronger, help the person develop and empower the development."

SOURCE: *Integrity* by Henry Cloud (Collins, 2006).

expectations being met? If the individual you're talking to is particularly difficult to work with, she might give you tremendous insight into what makes her act the way she does. If you spend at least twice as much time asking and listening as you do talking and telling, you will learn a great deal of valuable information.

> "Rarely are the protestations or accusations coming from the so-called difficult person the whole story behind their vitriol."
>
> —Robert Waite,
> CEO of Metal Sales Manufacturing Corporation

To frame your conversation, go back to the five basic questions that journalists use to gather the news.

Who? Other than you and your employee, others may be involved—your employee's coworkers, vendors, even customers. Who are the people affecting this person's job, and who does this person affect?

What? What are your subordinate's short-term and ongoing responsibilities? What are your responsibilities as a boss? Is there any miscommunication about responsibilities or expectations between the two of you?

WORK **FLOW** TOOLS

CONSTRUCTIVE CONFRONTATION CYCLE

Engage difficult employee in conversation.

↓

Create a written covenant.

↓

Schedule and conduct regular feedback and monitoring sessions.

↓

Celebrate the accomplishment of short-term goals.

↓

Repeat process until long-term goals have been achieved.

Where? Where is the subordinate supposed to be at any given time? Is attendance or lateness an issue? Is the subordinate expected to travel?

Dos & Don'ts ☑

MANAGING A DIFFICULT PERSON
As you move through the steps of constructive confrontation with a difficult employee, it's up to you to demonstrate through your attitude, words, and actions the behavior you would like to see. In your dealings with subordinates, coworkers, and superiors, you should be modeling what you expect from others.

☐ Do express your expectations in a reasonable way.

☐ Do live by the rules you make for others.

☐ Do initiate constructive conversations.

☐ Don't fail to put commitments in writing as covenants.

☐ Don't neglect to challenge your workers to follow through on their covenants.

☐ Do provide regular feedback.

Does the subordinate support team members in remote locations?

When? When is your subordinate required to complete tasks and communicate with supervisors—deadlines, reports, and so on? Schedule regular constructive feedback sessions in which you and your subordinate can review whether you are both on task, on schedule, on budget, and on track.

Why? Why are you having this conversation with the subordinate? Make sure you clarify the new goals you've set out to achieve and your reasons for requesting the employee to make changes.

How? How is your subordinate going to meet your new expectations? Discuss new approaches she might try to get her job done and to get along with others. Also offer encouragement and tell her how, as manager, you're going to support her efforts.

TAKING IT ON

Most people avoid dealing with difficult people, but one of the surest ways to get your career off and running is to do the things other people don't want to do. In this case, the people who succeed are those who are willing to roll up their sleeves and do the tough and often unpleasant work of dealing with difficult people.

THE BOTTOM LINE

Step Two: Covenant

Once you've had a constructive conversation with a difficult person and covered the basic questions, it's time to draft a covenant. Have your subordinate write up the basic agreement about what he will do to fulfill his obligations to the organization, including improving his difficult behavior. The covenant clearly sets out who?, what?, when?, where?, why?, and how? You want to engage the subordinate in the process of creating this document, so he doesn't feel the "covenant" is imposed by you. The covenant

CASE *FILE*

E-RECOGNITION

Offering recognition is a powerful tool for turning around negative attitudes in difficult people. One way to recognize positive behavior is allowing employees to shine a light on their peers' contributions. Wells Fargo Bank, for instance, has a great peer-to-peer electronic praise program called "E-wards" that allows any employee to recognize any other employee for doing a great job. Employees can send online thank you cards or e-cards to anyone they want to in the organization, and the system automatically sends a copy to a special "recognition mailbox" for tracking purposes. Those being thanked are entered into a quarterly is your working agreement on realistic and mutually agreed upon job responsibilities and behaviors. You and your employee sign off on it.

Step Three: Feedback

Every week, schedule a regular feedback session with your subordinate in her office. At these check-in sessions, confront the action items in the covenant, not the person.

You must hold your feedback sessions at specific, prearranged times and at designated intervals (e.g., weekly meetings). If you've kept good records of your initial conversation and have a written covenant with the difficult

---

drawing for prizes. Wells Fargo also awards e-wards to employees nominated by their peers. The electronic award is sent for approval to the nominee's manager, who receives a certificate with the details of the employee's achievement, a scratch-off ticket for a gift worth between $50 and $250 for the e-ward recipient, and a sheet that provides ideas on how to best present the award based on the recipient's preferences. In its first year, 1,600 e-cards were sent and 900 e-wards were distributed in the organization.

SOURCE: "Tip of the Week" by Bob Nelson, www.nelson-motivation.com (October 9, 2006).

employee, you'll have all the documentation necessary to check progress against the expectations that you've mutually agreed upon. Monitor how much your employee's performance and behavior have improved and continue to document this progress. If you need to initiate disciplinary or termination proceedings with your subordinate, you will have a well-documented case. Yet if you clearly articulate your expectations and

"To work effectively with a truly difficult person, or to have compassion for someone who does unpopular things, you must come to accept that you are also capable of doing unpopular things."

—Dr. Beth Langhorst, developmental psychologist

use constructive confrontation immediately to address problems with a difficult employee, it is unlikely that it will come to that.

Step Four: Celebration

Rewarded behavior is repeated behavior. If you want something good to happen more often, recognize it when it does happen. When creating a covenant with a difficult employee, you should not only discuss the employee's expectations and goals, but also discuss how the employee will be recognized for achieving particular milestones. There are thousands of ways to reward employees and most of them are extremely affordable and effective. (For specific advice on how to reward employees, contact the National Association for Employee Recognition at www.recognition.org.)

The BIG Picture

THE GOLDEN RULE

If you treat someone respectfully, they will respond in kind. The John Wayne days of putting on a gruff exterior so that people will fear you are long gone. If you belittle or intimidate people, they will usually resent rather than respect you.

The best way to show your respect for someone is to listen. Listen and then offer feedback about what you've heard.

Celebrations serve several purposes in the constructive confrontation cycle. First, they mark an ending and bring a sense of accomplishment. Second, celebrations are times to reflect on what

THINK BEFORE YOU HIT "SEND"

It is often easy to hide behind e-mail or to fire off a message impulsively. Don't give in to the temptation to send caustic messages when you are frustrated by a difficult person. Instead, try these strategies:

- Vent by writing a caustic e-mail, but don't send it.

- Reread every e-mail you plan to send about a touchy subject before you actually send it.

- Wait a day and reread the e-mail before sending it.

- Get a second opinion from a trusted source about whether you should send it.

- Begin your e-mail with your best intentions and end by suggesting next steps.

SOURCE: *Dealing with People You Can't Stand* by Rick Brinkman and Rick Kirschner (McGraw Hill, 2002).

THE BOTTOM LINE

has been accomplished to date and what still lies ahead. Third, they are springboards for the next phase. Higher productivity and increased performance will be built upon the success of past accomplishments.

PROGRESSIVE DISCIPLINE

If you have been engaged in constructive confrontation with an employee who continues to be difficult, it's time to use the extensive counseling and documentation you've built up to begin a formal program of progressive discipline. Progressive discipline offers difficult employees a chance to turn their situation around, under the looming threat of dismissal.

Reprimands

If you have dealt with the difficult person in your department with an approach such as constructive confrontation, and his behavior is still seriously disruptive, it is time to consider a formal reprimand. A reprimand clearly states what behavior is considered unacceptable and what the consequences are of such unacceptable behavior. Reprimands should not be temper tantrums or public displays of your authority. Reprimands are specific warnings and are always delivered in private. When giving a reprimand, you should explain to the difficult employee that termination is a possibility.

You do not have to wait for outright misconduct, such as negligence, insubordination, or an unwillingness to perform job requirements, to threaten to discipline. If an employee disrupts

• POWER POINTS •

GIVING FORMAL REPRIMANDS

Constructive confrontation can eliminate the need for formal reprimands, but sometimes you have no choice. If you have tried to address a problem and the employee's difficult behavior continues, any reprimand or communication from then on must be documented according to your human resources department's standards.

- Tell reprimanded employees that if they do not improve they will receive disciplinary action, which could include termination.

- Make each feedback session with an employee a performance review.

operations in any way, whether or not there has been prior counseling about the problem, you can move to the reprimand stage.

Your difficult employee might respond well to a serious reprimand. A message that says, "This is strike one in your file" could be all it takes for him to understand that you're serious and that you will use your institutional power to remove him if his behavior doesn't change.

It's a good idea to have a witness, such as a human resources representative, when giving reprimands. Since a difficult employee might

Set clear and measurable expectations for improvement at each session.

- If performance improves, offer positive feedback in public. However, deliver any reprimands for lack of improvement in private.

- If improvement is not made within an agreed on period of time, the countdown begins. Give the employee three chances to turn his behavior around.

- If the employee does not succeed on the third try, begin the termination process.

continue to challenge your authority, you should also have a specific, written action plan for improvement to accompany every reprimand and have your difficult person sign it. By documenting what was agreed upon, these written sign-offs help avoid future disputes.

Unlike constructive confrontations and most coaching, which are best held in your subordinate's workspace, oral reprimands should be delivered in your office. You need to demonstrate, in the most positive and affirming way, that you are the boss. In a reprimand, you use

Dos & Don'ts ☑

DELIVERING A REPRIMAND

When reprimanding a difficult person, as in all your dealings with employees, you must be careful to preserve the person's dignity. Here are some basic guidelines to follow:

- [ ] Do focus on the problem.
- [ ] Don't attack the individual personally—stick to the undesirable behavior.
- [ ] Do make sure that your position is supported by human resources or your superiors.
- [ ] Do document everything you do.
- [ ] Don't confuse your employee by sending mixed or conflicting messages about his performance.

your institutional authority to defend the best interests of the company.

When delivering an oral reprimand, you can't just tell a difficult employee that he is causing trouble and needs to shape up. You must be specific. Start preparing for the conversation by gathering all the information you need. Who is being affected and how? What exactly is the difficult person doing that disrupts the organization?

CASE *FILE*

DOCUMENTING PROBLEMS WITH A DIFFICULT MANAGER

Beverly Kelly, a human resources manager for Charles Lesser & Co., a 30-person California real estate consulting and strategic advisory firm, heard snippets of a conversation in the company lunch room about a manager's verbal abuse. Kelly needed to determine if these employees were being subjected to a "hostile work environment" and, if so, to respond on the company's behalf.

Kelly asked the complaining workers to put their grievances in writing. When their memos confirmed what she had heard, she issued a formal written reprimand that was placed in the manager's file. The manager was enrolled in a training course to teach him how to behave properly and professionally.

SOURCE: "Censored! 'Free' Speech at Work" by Scott Hays, *Workforce Management* (September 1, 1999).

Why is this employee behaving out of line? How can the issue best be remedied? These points should all be addressed in the oral reprimand.

Make an outline of the points you want to make to guide you through the conversation.

Then, based on this outline, create a formal written reprimand that incorporates all your facts. Ask for feedback from someone in human resources or from your boss.

When delivering the oral reprimand, don't stray from the issues. Don't allow the difficult employee to lead the conversation or shift the responsibility to a coworker or even back on you. The written record of the oral reprimand will keep you focused and on point. Get the difficult employee to sign a copy when you are finished.

Plan

SEEK A SEPARATION

Just because someone didn't work out in your department or under your leadership doesn't mean that she couldn't still be valuable to your organization. Many people who are difficult are actually fish out of water. For whatever reason, they wind up in a job that does not suit their skills. In this case, it makes sense to consider moving them, if possible. You can consult with human resources about other opportunities within your company that would be a better fit. One word of caution: be sure there is sufficient distance between her new department and yours.

Still, it is important for other employees to know that something is being done to deal with the difficult person. Your credibility as a boss suffers if people think you're not pursuing a solution to the problems the difficult person presents. Conversely, you gain credibility as a leader by attacking a problem and demonstrating your effectiveness in tough situations.

Without identifying people by name in public forums or making specific references, you can publicly acknowledge that you are "actively involved in making the workplace more productive." You can say you're working on an individual basis to solve problems and develop strengths wherever possible. Use these occasions to solicit feedback about general conditions in the workplace from everyone who works for you and ask for their suggestions. You might receive recommendations that are truly helpful.

TERMINATION

Firing someone is difficult on several levels. "Have I done the right thing?" many bosses wonder. Some are also nervous about the procedures. Others fear making a mistake that will cause aggravation and expense. It's better to err on the side of caution with something as important as terminating an employee. But once you have made the decision to terminate someone and you have documented evidence to support your decision, it's time to act.

First, consult one last time with human resources or your company lawyer. What comes next is a highly choreographed sequence of specific procedures determined by your human resources and legal departments that will terminate the difficult person's employment with your firm. It's critical that you follow the steps in the proper sequence. This accomplishes several goals, one of which is to protect you and your employer from the threat of litigation. You will also be allowing your soon-to-be-ex-employee to make a gracious and dignified exit.

Remember, there are few more stressful events in life than the loss of a job. Do get advice from

CASE *FILE*

TERMINATION HONORS THOSE LEFT BEHIND

Fred, the head of production for a tape duplication company in Southern California, was well-liked around the office. But when customers returned an excessive amount of cassettes because of poor recording quality, an internal review revealed that Fred was not properly monitoring the tape duplication machines because he was distracted by talking with fellow workers. After several failed attempts to get him to pay better attention to quality control, management gave him a chance to put his socializing impulse to work in sales and customer service.

Still, Fred never sold anything because he seemed far more interested in having your boss or from human resources about the finer points of the termination session and have all the details at your fingertips before you begin. Allow time between making the decision and telling the employee. It may take time to requisition and receive the employee's last check, for instance. You want to have check in hand before you tell the employee she's fired.

Many companies use sophisticated outplacement services that help terminated or laid-off employees find new work. If outplacement is possible through your company, discuss it with human resources as you plan the termination.

personal conversations than in selling. When he failed to respond to repeated (and well-documented) coaching and training opportunities, it became clear that Fred wasn't going to be productive in any area of the company. The problem was not so much that Fred wasn't doing his job as much as the fact that everyone else in the company knew Fred wasn't doing his job. Management had no choice but to terminate, despite their liking Fred very much. To not do so would have shown disrespect for the other employees who were working hard and contributing positively to the company.

SOURCE: *First Break All the Rules* by Marcus Buckingham (Simon & Schuster, 1999).

Approaching the Employee

Send a written invitation (or an e-mail with read receipt requested) to the employee you are about to terminate, detailing exactly when you want her to be in your office or a conference room in the human resources department that you have prearranged. Invite your human resources representative as well. The best time to deliver the news is at the end of a work day, perhaps even on a Friday. That way the terminated employee won't be humiliated by walking out in front of others.

Although a security presence usually isn't necessary, you should alert the person in charge of this function in your company. You may want to have someone standing by to ensure that the terminated employee leaves the premises peacefully.

The Termination Session

This session will be intentionally brief and you need to stay focused. As soon as your employee arrives, invite her to sit. Close the door and introduce the human resources representative, if she and the employee have not met. As soon as you sit down, tell the difficult employee that the decision has been made to terminate her employment with the organization. You're past the discussion stage.

This isn't a time to engage in idle talk nor is it time to debate the merit or lack of merit in terminating this person's employment. That was all discussed during your constructive confrontations or in the sequence of reprimands, when everything was clearly spelled out. Now it's time to part ways, as professionally as possible, trying to preserve everyone's dignity. The big decision has been made and you are now simply announcing it.

Say you are sorry that she didn't work out in your organization and wish her luck in her next position. Explain that you have her final check. Before turning over the check to her, present the termination paperwork for her to sign. This document will contain guarantees that the terminated employee will not engage in any form of backlash against you or the company, such as lawsuits or slander. Provide information about outplacement assistance, if you're offering it.

Once the paperwork is signed and the check is handed over, conclude the meeting and stand up. Offer your hand to shake, but be prepared to withdraw it gracefully if the person refuses. Escort the person back to her work area to gather her personal possessions.

Next Steps

Although the difficult employee has now been terminated and is off the premises, your work is not quite finished. You need to announce to the rest of your people that the employee is gone. Call a special meeting, perhaps the following morning, if a staff meeting is not already scheduled. If anyone has issues with or wants to discuss the matter, make yourself available privately for a limited amount of time, perhaps the balance of that week, to discuss it. Let them know that your decision to terminate or reassign the difficult person was, in many ways, a show of support for the dedicated hard work of the rest of your staff. You did it for their welfare as well as the overall best interests of the organization.

"No one deserves to live or work in fear of anyone. . . . Saying bye-bye is the best revenge."

—Frank Pacetta,
author of *Stop Whining–And Start Winning*

Termination is easier if you know you've done everything you can to save the relationship. Still, you may feel guilty about terminating the person, even someone who has made your life miserable. Yet, there are good reasons to follow the course of action you've chosen. Don't deny that your emotions are involved when dealing with difficult people. But don't allow your emotions to get in the way or lead you toward decisions and actions you will regret.

WHAT IF THE PROBLEM IS YOUR BOSS OR A PEER?

When the difficult person in your life is a peer, your boss, or your boss's boss, use all the tools available to you to guide your actions toward the most reasonable and sensible solution. Many employers do have a formal grievance process that allows an employee to express concerns about his manager or a coworker without fear of reprisal. Most companies' policies encourage the employee and the manager or coworker to work out the differences collaboratively before the process escalates. If this is not possible, the employee is usually required to take his grievance through a defined chain of command. The human resources department often plays mediator in any dispute that cannot be resolved.

In the end, sometimes your own departure is the best course. When it comes to such an extreme measure, make sure you've used sound judgment and not acted purely on emotion.

Disagreement—or Illegal Behavior?

If you have difficulty with a manager or a coworker, it is generally best to request a meeting with the other person and discuss the problem in an unemotional way. Be diplomatic. The objective is to reach a solution, not to get embroiled in an argument that will only make matters worse.

"Difficulty" can be broadly defined as any work dispute, personality conflict, or other problem that makes it unpleasant to interact with another person. A manager or coworker is not breaking any law by exhibiting hostility, shouting, or even verbally abusing an employee, even though this behavior may be inappropriate. However, the verbal abuse could constitute illegal behavior if it involves a racial or religious slur or sexual harassment of any kind. Any physical abuse could be illegal.

Document any questionable or disturbing interaction with a boss or coworker by writing down the date, the nature of the interaction, and, if possible, the specific words the person said. Note the names of any witnesses present during the incident. Next, find out what your employer's policy is on voicing complaints about bosses or coworkers. If the company has a grievance process, follow the steps for making a formal complaint. If there is no grievance process, seek advice from the human resources department.

If you are convinced that the difficulty or disagreement involves something illegal, such as discrimination on the grounds of race, gender, or age, it is likely you will need to seek legal advice. To have a legitimate case, you'll need documentation in the form of notes, e-mails, or other written documents, along with statements from any witnesses.

Your Legal Rights

Employees' rights are protected by federal labor laws and, in some cases, state laws, when it comes to discrimination, sexual harassment, and unfair labor practices. The National Labor Relations Act (NLRA) and other statutes provide some protection for employees to speak out under certain

CASE *FILE*

WORKPLACE BULLYING

Celia G. Zimmerman filed a pregnancy discrimination complaint against her employer, Direct Federal Credit Union in Massachusetts, and its CEO, David Breslin. After she notified Breslin that she intended to pursue the claim in court, Zimmerman said her employer took retaliatory action. She said Breslin publicly made disparaging remarks about her, ignored her attempts to participate in meetings, biased members of the credit union's board against her, and intimidated employees who sided with her.

Zimmerman lost the case against her employer for discrimination but won on her claim of retaliation. The judge said, "Such actions quite simply cannot be viewed as falling either within the legitimate scope of a corporate officer's employment or within the corporation's legitimate interests."

SOURCE: "Verdict for Workplace Bullying Is Upheld" by Wendy L. Pfaffenbach, *Massachusetts Lawyers Weekly* (November 27, 2000).

conditions. For example, employees who are part of a union may complain through the union, and they may engage in collective bargaining, boycotts, and strikes.

The **BIG** Picture

EMPLOYMENT AT WILL
One of the reasons you need to be
diplomatic in dealing with a boss or
coworker who is difficult is the lack
of a single wrongful termination law.
Basically, anyone who is employed on
an "at-will" basis (which means there
is no employment contract) can be
terminated at any time. Since most
people are employed at will, employers can generally terminate them even
without cause. The only restrictions are
those put in place by federal laws (the
laws prohibiting discrimination, for
example) and those in contracts (such
as a collective bargaining agreement);
ignoring these restrictions when firing
someone would constitute so-called
wrongful termination. From a practical
perspective, most employers wish to
maintain good relationships between
managers and employees, so there are
provisions in place for handling whatever disputes and disagreements arise.
Nonetheless, you should be cautious
in bringing up complaints and be sure
to follow any procedures your employer
has established.

There are also other statutes that provide "whistle-blower" protection to an employee who reports an employer's illegal activity, refuses to disobey a law, testifies against an employer, or complains about sexual harassment.

What happens, however, when an employee has complaints about a difficult boss or coworker? Here, the employee's legal rights are much less defined. If an employee speaks out in ways that constitute insubordination or disobedience, the employer is generally within its rights to terminate the individual.

In fact, if there is no employment contract, an employer can terminate an employee for almost any cause, as long as it is not discriminatory. For a termination to be considered unlawful, the employee must be able to prove that the employer discriminated against her.

Managers will always have to deal with the problem of difficult people. It can be one of the most demanding—and trickiest—challenges a manager faces. Although each case is as individual as each personality, identifying typical patterns of difficult behavior and recognizing some of the underlying causes will help you, as manager, to address them. Always remember that your biggest concern is how to use your institutional authority to honor and protect the efforts of all your other hard-working, dedicated employees.

Off and Running >>>

You are now ready to put what you have learned from this book into practice. Use this section as a review guide:

CHAPTER 1.
HOW DIFFICULT PEOPLE AFFECT THE WORKPLACE

- Difficult people affect your productivity on all levels.

- Difficult people waste valuable time and energy by shifting your attention and focus onto them.

- Ask yourself: Is this person wasting his or her own time, other people's time, or the company's money or resources?

- A difficult person can diminish energy and enthusiasm in the workplace, causing departmental success to suffer.

- Communication (especially when questions or problems arise) helps avoid the unrealistic expectations that can cause resentment.

- Observing and maintaining boundaries is an important component of a comfortable working environment.

- Difficult people are everywhere. It's best to learn how to cope with them successfully.

CHAPTER 2.
UNDERSTANDING DIFFICULT PEOPLE

- Understanding what makes a difficult person tick is critical. There are simple ways to avoid conflict that can make the difference between a satisfactory employee and a difficult employee.

- As a manager, it is important to identify the key traits of difficult people and to learn ways to manage them without being distracted from your overall goals.

- There are ten types of difficult people commonly found in the workplace: the Slave Driver, the Black Hole, the Minutiae Monster, the Busybody, the Recluse, the Bully, the Liar, the Outlaw, the Blamer-Complainer, and the Know-It-All.

Off and Running >>>

- Learning to work effectively with a difficult boss or coworker can improve productivity in the workplace. Just because a person is "difficult," doesn't mean that he or she won't have something to contribute.

- Don't feel you have to immediately take on whatever the Slave Driver hands you. Focus on what is most important. Sit down with the over-delegating Slave Driver to analyze and prioritize your workload.

- When dealing with the needy Black Hole, take the initiative, encourage moving ahead, bring him into the group, and build confidence.

- Send the Minutiae Monster the message that doing something in a reasonable amount of time is as important as doing it right.

- Give the Busybody productive activities that satisfy her need for interaction; assign her a research or reporting task to make efficient use of her natural curiosity.

- Tread lightly with the Recluse, who may be shy or lack social skills; usually the Recluse does more than his share of work.

- Divert a Bully's energies elsewhere by giving him a responsibility at which he can excel. Cordial interactions and increased confidence will soothe a Bully, making him less severe.

- If you suspect you are dealing with a Liar, don't rely on your memory of incidents or statements; write everything down so that you have documentation when it is needed.

- The Outlaw's questioning of authority might not necessarily be a bad thing; if her aim is to improve the status quo, encourage creativity, not compliance.

- Acknowledge that mistakes are a fact of life, but reward problem solvers; doing so will encourage Blamer-Complainers to change. Use Blamer-Complainer's critical eye to find holes in any documents or presentations that are being prepared.

Off and Running >>>

- Work with the Know-It-All's strengths by assigning him the job of creating a database, for example, which would play into his desire to be Information Central.

- It is key to open the lines of communication and to make sure that the difficult employee feels at ease communicating about problems on the job.

CHAPTER 3.
HOW TO HANDLE DIFFICULT PEOPLE

- Implement a system of constructive criticism so that small problems can be addressed and corrected before they become major problems.

- Give feedback to your employees so that you can monitor their progress and encourage any changes or improvements.

- Respect can go a long way. Sometimes a difficult employee is feeling disrespected, either by his coworkers or by his superiors, because of miscommunication.

- If the difficult person you face in the workplace is a boss or superior, try working your problems out diplomatically before moving ahead with a formal grievance process. Make sure you use good judgment and do not act upon your emotions. Remain level-headed and strong.

- To manage difficult people and the problems that come with them, separate the problem from the person.

- Use firing as a last resort; use constructive confrontation to resolve—or even prevent—conflicts and build coalitions.

- The four steps of constructive confrontation are: conversation, covenant drafting, giving feedback, and celebrating accomplishments.

- Reinforce the constructive confrontation cycle by repeating each step until long-term goals are achieved.

- Give positive feedback in public, but give reprimands in private.

Off and Running >>>

- Sometimes there is no other option but termination. Be as diplomatic as possible to avoid any further confrontation in your workplace. Trust that you are doing the right thing for your business and then make sure you follow all the correct procedures with the support of your human resources department.

- If you do need to terminate someone's employment, the best time is at the end of the workday, preferably at the end of the week; make a point to call a meeting the next workday to notify your other employees in person.

Recommended Reading

Snakes in Suits: When Psychopaths Go to Work
Paul Babiak, Ph.D., and Robert D. Hare, Ph.D.
A compelling look at how psychopaths work in the corporate environment—what kind of companies attract them, how they manipulate employees, and how they function day by day, while hiding within the corporate culture. It describes the subtle warning signs of psychopathic behavior and explains how managers can protect themselves and their companies.

The Transparent Leader: How to Build a Great Company Through Straight Talk, Openness, and Accountability
Herb Baum with Tammy Kling
In the wake of numerous corporate scandals, Baum offers business leaders a compelling method to get maximum results by being open and honest in business practices.

Leaders: Strategies for Taking Charge, 2nd ed.
Warren Bennis and Burt Nanus
Leadership guru Warren Bennis and his coauthor Burt Nanus reveal the four key principles every manager should know.

Reinventing Leadership: Strategies to Empower the Organization
Warren Bennis and Robert Townsend
Two of America's experts on leadership show how their strategies can lead organizations into a future of increased employee satisfaction and continued economic growth.

Leadership and the One Minute Manager: Increasing Effectiveness through Situational Leadership®
Ken Blanchard with Patricia Zigarmi and Drea Zigarmi
Best-selling author Blanchard, teaches managers how to use his patented method of Situational Leadership® to elicit the best performance from employees.

Coping with Difficult People: The Proven-Effective Battle Plan That Has Helped Millions Deal with the Troublemakers in Their Lives at Home and at Work
Robert M. Bramson
Based on 14 years of research and observation, Bramson's book shows how to cope with impossible people and presents the six basic steps that allow people to deal with just about anyone and reclaim power in any relationship.

Dealing with People You Can't Stand: How to Bring Out the Best in People at Their Worst
Dr. Rick Brinkman and Dr. Rick Kirschner
Brinkman and Kirschner identify and explore the psychological roots of ten specific behavior patterns.

The Success Principles™: How to Get from Where You Are to Where You Want to Be
Jack Canfield with Janet Switzer
One of the coauthors of the incredibly successful Chicken Soup for the Soul series provides the principles and strategies to meet a wide variety of goals.

Dealing with Difficult People: How to Deal with Nasty Customers, Demanding Bosses and Annoying Co-workers
Roberta Cava
This book offers proven techniques for working with others, reducing stress, and increasing confidence and enthusiasm in professional relationships.

Integrity: The Courage to Meet the Demands of Reality
Henry Cloud
Dr. Cloud explores the six qualities of character that define integrity. He uses stories from well-known business leaders and sports figures to illustrate each of these qualities.

Since Strangling Isn't an Option: Dealing with Difficult People—Common Problems and Uncommon Solutions
Sandra A. Crowe
This revealing book offers practical and realistic solutions for dealing with difficult people and avoiding habits that provoke negative behaviors.

The Daily Drucker: 366 Days of Insight and Motivation for Getting the Right Things Done
Peter F. Drucker with Joseph A. Maciariello
Widely regarded as the greatest management thinker of modern times, Drucker here offers his penetrating and practical wisdom with his trademark clarity, vision, and humanity.

The Effective Executive
Peter F. Drucker
Drucker shows how to "get the right things done," demonstrating the distinctive skill of the executive and offering fresh insights into old and seemingly obvious business situations.

Innovation and Entrepreneurship
Peter F. Drucker
This is the classic business tome for presenting innovation and entrepreneurship as a purposeful and systematic discipline. This practical book explains what all businesses and institutions have to know, learn, and do in today's market.

Corps Business: The 30 Management Principles of the U.S. Marines
David H. Freedman
Freedman examines the organization and culture of the United States Marine Corps and relates how business enterprises could benefit from such Marine values as sacrifice, perseverance, integrity, commitment, and loyalty.

Toxic Emotions at Work: How Compassionate Managers Handle Pain and Conflict
Peter J. Frost
Frost explains why and how managers and leaders cause emotional pain and explores ways in which managers can prevent it from becoming a toxic agent in the workplace.

Common Sense Business: Starting, Operating, and Growing Your Small Business in Any Economy!
Steve Gottry
This book tells you how to succeed throughout every phase of the small business life cycle. Author Gottry offers practical application in the real world of small business.

A Survival Guide for Working with Humans: Dealing with Whiners, Back-Stabbers, Know-It-Alls, and Other Difficult People
Gini Graham Scott
This guide to managing relationships with coworkers describes how difficult people can affect one's ability to get the job done—and even one's long-term success—and offers real-life techniques for handling common situations at work.

How to Work for an Idiot: Survive and Thrive . . . without Killing your Boss
John Hoover
Organizational behavior and executive therapist Dr. Hoover teaches readers how to handle all types of bad bosses.

"Yes" or "No": The Guide to Better Decisions
Spencer Johnson, M.D.
Best-selling author Spencer Johnson presents a practical system anyone can use to make better decisions, soon and often—in both one's professional and personal life.

What Really Works: The 4+2 Formula for Sustained Business Success
William Joyce, Nitin Nohria, and Bruce Roberson
Based on a groundbreaking 5-year study, analyzing data on 200 management practices, *What Really Works* reveals the effectiveness of practices that really matter.

The Wisdom of Teams: Creating the High Performance Organization
Jon R. Katzenbach and Douglas K. Smith
Authors Katzenbach and Smith reveal the most important element in team success, who excels at team leadership, and why companywide change depends on teams.

You Can't Win a Fight with Your Boss: & 55 Other Rules for Success
Tom Markert
This guide to surviving the pitfalls of the modern corporate environment presents 56 practical rules that one can use to find corporate success.

Executive Intelligence: What All Great Leaders Have
Justin Menkes
In this thought-provoking volume, Menkes pinpoints the cognitive skills needed to excel in senior management positions.

The Corporate Coach: How to Build a Team of Loyal Customers and Happy Employees
James B. Miller with Paul B. Brown
Founder and CEO of Miller Business Systems, Jim Miller shows how giving customers legendary services and also motivating employees make for a winning combination.

In Search of Excellence: Lessons from America's Best-Run Companies
Thomas J. Peters and Robert H. Waterman, Jr.
Based on a study of 43 of America's best-run companies, *In Search of Excellence* describes eight basic principles of management that made these organizations successful.

Quiet Leadership: Six Steps to Transforming Performance at Work
David Rock
Rock demonstrates how to be a quiet leader, master at bringing out the best performance in others, by improving the way people process information.

The Addictive Organization: Why We Overwork, Cover Up, Pick Up the Pieces, Please the Boss, and Perpetuate Sick Organization
Anne Wilson Schaef and Diane Fassel
Schaef and Fassel show how managers and workers exhibit the classic symptoms of addiction: denying and avoiding problems, assuming that there is no other way of acting, and manipulating events to maintain the status quo.

*Radical Collaboration: Five Essential Skills to Overcome
Defensiveness and Build Successful Relationships*
James W. Tamm and Ronald J. Luyet
Tamm and Luyet argue that getting along with your colleagues or customers is imperative and collaborative skills
have never been more important. This how-to manual show
readers how to be more skillful at building relationships,

*The Cycle of Leadership: How Great Leaders Teach Their
Companies to Win*
Noel M. Tichy
Using examples from real companies, Tichy shows how
managers can begin to transform their own businesses into
teaching organizations and better-performing companies.

*Handling Difficult People: What to Do When People Push
Your Buttons*
Dr. John Townsend
Best-selling author Dr. John Townsend challenges readers to
stop responding to difficult people in ways that don't work
and helps them better understand what makes "button push-
ers" act the way they do—and why.

Winning
Jack Welch with Suzy Welch
Devoted to the real "stuff" of work and packed with personal
anecdotes, this book offers deep insights, original thinking,
and solutions to nuts-and-bolts problems.

*Taking Charge When You're Not in Control: A Practical
Approach to Getting What You Want Out of Life*
Patricia Wiklund, Ph.D.
Nationally renowned psychotherapist and author Patricia
Wiklund explains how to get a grip on life and its troubles to
gain a sense of well-being and control.

Index